Citizenship under Fire

Citizenship under Fire

DEMOCRATIC EDUCATION
IN TIMES OF CONFLICT

Sigal R. Ben-Porath

PRINCETON UNIVERSITY PRESS

PRINCETON AND OXFORD

Second printing, and first paperback printing, 2009
Paperback ISBN: 978-0-691-14111-4

The Library of Congress has cataloged the cloth edition of this book as follows

Ben-Porath, Sigal R., 1967–
Citizenship under fire : democratic education in times of conflict /
Sigal R. Ben-Porath.
p. cm.
Includes bibliographical references and index.
ISBN-13: 978-0-691-12434-6 (hardcover : alk. paper)
ISBN-10: 0-691-12434-5 (hardcover : alk. paper)
1. Citizenship—Study and teaching. 2. War and education.
3. Educational change. I. Title.
LC1091.B39 2006
370.11′5—dc22
2005023254

British Library Cataloging-in-Publication Data is available

This book has been composed in Palatino

Printed on acid-free paper. ∞

press.princeton.edu

Printed in the United States of America

2 3 4 5 6 7 8 9 10

TO MY PARENTS

SHLOMIT AND PELEG RADAY

Contents

Acknowledgments

THE EFFECTS OF conflict on citizenship and education preoccupied my thoughts long before my scholarly interest in the topic evolved. As a high school student in Israel, I was unsettled by the narrow perspectives of history the curriculum addressed. As a young woman I was struck by the imbalanced effects a protracted conflict has across gender lines. When I began teaching history and civic studies in a high school, I realized that the school system was supporting the social struggle for endurance but simultaneously—and perhaps inadvertently—hindering the development of fresh perspectives that could induce peace and thereby failing to inspire democratic attitudes. I was lucky to have had the professional opportunity to study these matters more methodically.

During 2000–2001 I participated in a fascinating interdisciplinary research group in Israel, expertly led by Meron Benvenisti and supported by the Ford Foundation. The Truman Institute at the Hebrew University of Jerusalem provided the venue for the meetings. The group worked on a project, optimistically titled "The Morning After," concerning the various challenges Israeli society would face the morning after peace arrived. The outstanding scholarly environment in which these thoughts and normative arguments were formed is evident to me in many pages of the current work. For that I wish to thank Meron Benvenisti, Nimrod Goren, Shlomit Raday, and the other participants of The Morning After group. Our works were collected in a book published in Hebrew.

I did most of the work on this book during a postdoctoral fellowship at Princeton University's Center for Human Values. I am grateful to the Spencer Foundation and Tel Aviv University for grants that enabled me to write this book. My deepest gratitude is to Amy Gutmann, whose advice, support, and trust are an ongoing source of encouragement.

I have presented parts of this work during the years 2002–2005 at the annual meetings of the American Political Science Association, the Midwest Political Science Association, the Philosophy of Education Society, and the North American Society for Social Philosophy. I thank the participants and commentators, especially Tim McDonough and Michael Walzer. Some of the ideas in chapter 1 were presented at the Diversity within Unity conference at Oxford in 2000. A version of chapter 6 was presented at the Human Rights Fund lecture at the University of Nebraska—Lincoln; I thank Jeff Spinner-Halev for inviting me to give this lecture, as well as for his friendly advice and scholarly perspective. At the University of Pennsylvania I was invited to present this work by the international and comparative student group at the Graduate School of Education; I thank them for the invitation and for their productive comments on my work. I wish to thank my Penn colleagues Kathy Hall, John Puckett, and Kathy Shultz for their support and advice. Some of the critical discussions of literature in chapter 3 appeared in *Philosophy of Education*, in a review essay titled "War and Peace Education."

Chapter 4 is an expanded and revised version of an article that was presented at the 1998 IAPh meeting; it will be published in the volume *Identities and Differences*, eds. Deborah Orr and Diana Taylor (Rowman & Littlefield, forthcoming). Chapter 5 is an expanded and revised version of an article titled "Multicultural Education, Peace, and Democracy," which appeared in the *Philosophy of Education Yearbook*, 2005. Chapter 6 is an expanded and revised version of an article titled "Radicalizing Democratic Education" which appeared in the *Philosophy of Education Yearbook*, 2003. Both chapters 5 and 6 appear here with the permission of the Philosophy of Education Society.

I am fortunate to have a number of wonderful scholars as friends, who devoted time and thought to my project and specific arguments within it, provided me with ever more books to read on the topic, and encouraged me to keep working. Some of these friends read drafts of the book or of some chapters, and their comments pushed me to further develop my views. It is my pleasure to thank Harry Brighouse, Suzanne Dovi, Meira Levinson, Rob Reich, Rogers Smith, Yuli Tamir, and Mariah Zeisberg for commenting on parts or all of this book, and offering me invaluable advice on the arguments presented here. I also thank my editor, Ian Malcolm.

I am indebted as well to the Immigration and Naturalization Service, which provided me and my two children—not without a good fight—with the opportunity to experience wartime citizenship not only in Israel but also in the United States.

Many of the ideas in this book were developed through lengthy discussions with my husband, Eran Ben-Porath. This book would not have been the same without his willingness to lend me his ear, his mind, and his excellent editorial abilities. Making the time and space for writing is a heavy task that must be undertaken by all family members, and thus any credit for this work should be shared with Eran, Itamar, and Amalia.

This book is dedicated with love to my father, who taught me that democracy needs to be struggled for; and to my mother, who showed me the importance of being engaged in what we care about, both politically and personally.

Citizenship under Fire

Introduction

IN THE SUMMER OF 2002, Israeli high school students took their final exams for their high school diplomas. At age seventeen or eighteen, just before gaining their voting rights and beginning their mandatory military service, these students were confronted with the following question on their civic studies exam: "Explain why conscientious objection is subversive."

With a stroke of a pen, the exam writers had abandoned decades of democratic deliberation on the balance between conscience and compliance, between majority rule and minority dissent. The students were presented with the conclusion, veiling a demand to refrain from joining the ranks of soldiers who, in the preceding months, had refused to serve in the occupied territories. At a culminating point of their civic education, the students were expected to be able to explain why opposing the decisions of a democratically elected government is, in the context of war, treacherous.

Civic education, democratic principles, peace and war are entangled in many ways. When a liberal democracy lives peacefully for a long period of time—as the United States did until September 11, 2001—the circumstances of peace become neutral. They move to the background, to be taken for granted, and they fail to draw the attention of citizens or to generate philosophical and political discussion. This failure is based on a misperception; as Susan Sontag pointedly maintains, "[T]hroughout history [w]ar has been the norm and peace the exception."[1] When such a democracy enters a period of war, many of the basic assumptions upon which its social order is constructed are distorted. Civic freedoms, long held as guaranteed, are suddenly limited. Social practices and personal priorities are revised. The education system cannot evade this fate. As public institutions responsible for preparing future generations to become part of society, schools are inclined to undergo change. This book explores some of these changes and offers a normative direction they should take, herein dubbed "expansive education."

1

Since September 2001, the American political and academic spheres have become absorbed in discussions of terrorism and war. With the one field trying to combat global terrorism and the other field struggling to understand it, little room is left for talk about democratic principles or visions of peace. Civic society and the public education system can reinforce this trend or contest it.

Having been raised through the seemingly endless Israeli-Palestinian conflict, I began thinking about civic education in wartime in the context of the Israeli political sphere and local public education system. I was challenged to generalize the concepts I was developing by some striking similarities in the post–9/11 American public sphere. Those analogous social processes generated by the sense of vulnerability that conflict produces are termed here "belligerent citizenship." The main examples used here are the Israeli and the contemporary American ones, but the conceptual framework is wider than these two examples. The conceptualization of belligerent citizenship offered in the first chapter is relevant to some extent, with necessary local modifications, to other democracies at war. Similarly, the need to respond educationally to the changing conceptions of citizenship is evident in countries beyond those used here to illustrate the theoretical suggestions. In addition, the relevance of the project goes beyond wartime alone. Expansive education, focusing on attitudes relevant for preserving democratic inclinations in wartime as well as for containing the social discord that peace and the road toward it are bound to bring, is an important part of the political education of future citizens in any contemporary democracy. Examining education in the context of war and the quest for peace, beyond its immediate relevance to countries at war, can help educators and political theorists focus their attention on crucial and often neglected components of civic education. The significance of teaching civic values lies in their contribution to achieving peace, but not in it alone. These civic values are one and the same as those required for political participation, for tolerant deliberation of the public agenda, as well as for facilitating civic equality. The values and attitudes endorsed by expansive education can support a democratic response to circumstances of social conflict and tensions, not only to those of international conflict (in many cases those two conditions can hardly be told apart). Therefore, the education system's responsibility is to introduce these values to children in order to give them an opportunity to become equal citizens in a democratic peaceful society, which they can help bring about.

I call the approach developed in this book "expansive education" because it is designed to respond to common, restrictive social tendencies of wartime. These tendencies are incongruous with the democratic ideal in that they work, illustratively, in opposing directions. Democracy aims at widening the circles of participation, extending the scope of public debate, and diversifying the questions asked and the opinions voiced. Common social responses to wartime—or belligerent citizenship—does the opposite. It narrows down the public agenda, the list of relevant questions and issues to be debated publicly, and the acceptable opinions that should be tolerated. The role of expansive education is to protect the democratic ideal against this social tide.

Relying on education to overcome war is a disputable choice. First, education is a long-term process; educating for peace might hint that peace as a political reality is far beyond the immediate future. Second, the education system is dependent upon the political system and is typically governed by elected officials; consequently, it is prone to reflecting the status quo rather than forming a revolutionary response to it. Finally, peace—like war—is by and large regarded as the business of politicians, to negotiate through diplomatic channels. War is not waged by pedagogues; it may seem that they have little power to overcome it. All these arguments stand in the background of prevalent policies regarding peace. In regions where conflict and war are an ongoing reality, individuals tend to develop perspectives that accommodate conflict as a normal aspect of social life; societies grow to accept conflict as given and often fail to envision alternatives.

It is indeed political leaders who take the decision to go to war, to avoid it, or to declare its end. But the culture of war or the commitment to peace can be cultivated only on the social rather than the political realm. The acceptance or rejection of war is the responsibility of individuals and communities. Opposing the tide on issues of war and peace can be arduous, even in a democracy. Although opponents to a democratic government are not readily executed or expatriated, they can still face a hostile response, fueled by a perceived necessity to unite in times of danger. Expansive education is constructed as a way for the education system to contribute to the construction of a democratic society committed to peace and prepared for the obstacles in the path leading to its achievement. It is based on a concept of citizenship that takes into account the challenges created by a state of conflict, and incorporates them into existing forms of democratic and civic education. Working toward a stronger commitment to the values underlying democracy and peace, in the context of countries engaged in conflicts and faced with security threats, can serve as a long-term investment in the future of democracy.

For a country and a society to endure a protracted conflict and possibly the road for peace, all the while maintaining democratic commitments and structures, it must respond educationally (that is, patiently and expansively) to the tensions and challenges they create. In times of conflict, leaders might relinquish democratic principles and practices in order to respond immediately and effectively to security needs. Expansive education can provide a framework for a civic response to such challenges to the democratic order in constructive ways. When striving for peace, leaders work to overcome mutual distrust and to dispel the concerns of groups within their respective constituencies; the attitudinal and perceptual preparation by educators committed to expansive education can support this political endeavor.

This book begins with an exploration of changes in the conceptions of citizenship in the context of war. The attitudes, perspectives, and capacities required to respond to security threats and promote peace are deeply embedded in society's conception of citizenship. Understanding the ways in which these conceptual changes and reproductions function, and differentiating their constructive from their potentially destructive components, are the first steps in developing an approach to civic education focused on a commitment to democracy and peace. Just War theory is the main political attempt to confront issues of justice in war. It is important to realize that social dimensions need to be added to the moral-political debate on Just War, to make it responsive to the differing needs of a democratic society involved in a protracted conflict. Expansive education is an attempt at outlining the educational dimension of the expanded Just War theory. In chapter 1 I demonstrate, borrowing mainly from the American and the Israeli experiences, how the background of conflict and fear creates shifts in common conceptions of citizenship. I consider the changes wartime generates in central aspects of democratic citizenship, namely, participation, deliberation, and social unity (or patriotism). The varying characteristics of citizenship in times of war and peace add up to a distinction between belligerent citizenship, which is typical of democracies in wartime, and the liberal-democratic citizenship that is characteristic of more peaceful democracies. I discuss how these changes make the conceptualization of citizenship as shared fate more plausible both descriptively and normatively than its conceptualization as identity.

The ways in which the education system responds to these changes generates the attitudes of the next generation of citizens, therefore replicating, or even accentuating, these conceptions into the future. In chapter 2 I consider how some educational practices might perpetuate belligerent conceptions. The contemporary debate on the teaching of patriotism in schools is considered in this context. I maintain that contemporary authors on this topic tend to disregard the consequences of their constructive theoretical approaches for peace and war. They thereby render the discussion of patriotic education less relevant during times when politicians, educators, and society in general are preoccupied with these matters and the educational system is hardpressed to respond. Most crucially, many theories tend to work against a presumed background of moral pluralism. In times of war, and particularly during a protracted conflict, societies tend to unite around common values such as (a narrow form of) patriotism and suppress ideological and other differences. They thus create circumstances that require a responsive consideration from democratic educational theories. Expansive education aims to offer tools for defending basic democratic values not only in the face of moral conflicts but also in the face of defensive unification and belligerent citizenship.

5

The conceptual and political exploration of the first two chapters, combined with my contention that the education system's moral role is to serve as an anchor for change, informs the next step. The next three chapters place expansive education within more specific theoretical contexts, responding to discussions in the subfields of peace education, feminist pedagogy, and multicultural education.

Chapter 3 examines contemporary discussions in peace education literature, pointing out two different trends in this field. On the one hand, peace education theorists subscribing to the "pedagogic trend" tend to portray a narrow conception of conflict and, as a result, focus on offering techniques of "conflict resolution" or "reduction of violence." These techniques represent a simplified conception of peace and of civil society's role in enabling it. These naïve conceptions stem from a tendency to strictly contrast peace with war and violence, and to neglect or overlook the civic components of each of these sociopolitical phenomena. Consequently, although this trend in peace education may offer ad hoc tools for responding to specific local tensions, it falls short of addressing the more general problem of sustaining society's democratic structure and its commitment to peace through times of conflict.

Contrary to this minimalist approach, theorists who subscribe to some version of the "holistic trend" misconceptualize peace education efforts by reconstructing all interpersonal and group relations as power struggles, and generally labeling all social interactions as forms of conflict. Such theorists err by concluding that peace is never an attainable—or even a desirable—option. Relying on Foucauldian and Frankfurt school theories, postmodernist peace education theorists deconstruct universal conceptions of the good, of human rights, and of peace itself, thereby undermining any attempt to improve society or to contribute to a realistic (rather than utopian) better future.

I critically examine these two prevalent trends of peace education and conclude that for peace education to be effective and defensible, it must take into account both the psycho-pedagogical and the political aspects of the quest for peace.

Chapter 4 examines the complex relations of gender and war from a civic education perspective. It begins by identifying some of the unique challenges that conflict poses before women, both practically and in regard to social perceptions. At the background of the discussion is an understanding of the mutual construction of gender and war, and its influence on women's lives during protracted conflicts. The responses of feminist thought to these challenges vary, and this chapter is focused on those that feed the main pedagogical approaches to the gendered challenges of war. Some of the pedagogic tools developed and employed by feminist educators are considered with suggestions for their adaptation into the context of civic education in wartime. The main conclusion of this chapter is that feminist pedagogy's potential inspiration to civic education goes far beyond the realm of gender relations. The strengths of feminist analyses of oppression and of gender-related challenges, and some suggested educational, social, and political responses, are reformulated and extended into the broader context of military conflict and the expansive education response.

Chapter 5 explores some prominent works on multicultural political and educational thought in light of their possible contribution to the objectives of expansive education. The attempt to overcome past wrongs has comparable aspects in intergroup and international conflict contexts. Consequently, some social and educational responses suggested by multicultural theorists can be adapted to the context of expansive education.

The chapter focuses on two key conceptions in multicultural thought, namely, the acknowledgment of past wrongs and forgiveness. Working against a background of oppressive unity rather than unwelcome diversity, these concepts are adapted to fit the educational needs of a democratic society at war.

In the sixth and concluding chapter, threads from the various approaches discussed are pulled to weave a more comprehensive description of expansive education. A robust civic education curriculum must be based on developing proper skills for facing the challenges of wartime as well as of the quest for peace. The commitment to democracy and peace that is generated through expansive education is a primary way to respond to the social challenges that arise in times of a protracted conflict, such as the decrease in social tolerance and the suspension of issues

and perspectives from the public agenda. The public deliberation of these issues through matters concerning curricular decisions, pedagogical concerns, and democratic education can encourage the general public as well as the students, as future
citizens, to create a broader common agenda. This process offers
an opportunity to practice civic skills and strengthen democratic
commitments while creating a hospitable atmosphere for peace
among subgroups within the democratic society as well as with
other nations.

The social circumstances of living with conflict in a democratic
society are rarely considered in contemporary educational theories. Consequently, the civil society's conception of peace is
vague and hardly carries with it practical and normative implications. Not only the potentiality of reaching peace, but also the
democratic nature of society itself, are at stake. The discussion
in this book is aimed at a nuanced understanding of the roles
that citizenship and civic education play in facilitating peace and
preserving democracy in times of conflict. Educational resources
devoted to creating a commitment to democracy and peace in
each country can support the endurance of democracy through
war. Civic and democratic commitments, interpreted according
to each country's set of cultural beliefs and traditions, can serve
as a counterweight for the culture of war that stems from global
tensions, terrorism, and the ensuing military conflicts. In this
way, expansive education can be hoped to contribute to creating
democratically committed citizens who maintain a realistic ap-
preciation of peace even in times of conflict.

Citizenship in Wartime

WHEN A DEMOCRACY enters a period of war or overt security threats, its citizens' lives are affected in many ways. Their feelings about their country can be transformed; public and political distinctions between "us" and "them" shift; citizens' expectations from the government can be revised in light of what they perceive as their most urgent interests. The public agenda often becomes preoccupied with security issues; the public sphere is rearranged around these newly defined focal points. Many issues, including immigration, criminal law, demography, free speech, and artistic expression, to name but a few, become part of the security discourse. Access to information about some of these matters is constrained accordingly. These changes can broadly be described as a shift from an open, democratic notion of citizenship to a narrow conception of the relations between state and individual, which I term "belligerent citizenship." This chapter will trace some of the basic alterations in the conceptualization of citizenship that occur in times of war or conflict, as a basis for constructing a qualified notion of civic education.

In democratic countries enjoying more peaceful times, citizenship is a multilayered conception that expresses the legal, social, and cultural relations between the state and its members.[1] Democratic conceptions of citizenship are aimed at coordinating the relations between individual and state, and balancing the state's power with individuals' rights.[2] Deliberative models analyze the communicative processes that allow for large populations to debate a host of topics that correspond with their shared interests; perfectionist theorists examine the core values that should be expressed in the structure of state institutions; multicultural and liberal theorists debate the extent to which the state should transfer decisional powers to subgroups and the ways in which it can still guarantee the protection of individual rights within those groups. Generally speaking, these various theories are concerned with designing processes that would allow individuals to flourish in the context of a democratic order.

Thus, the structure of the relations between the state and its members, as expressed by the notion of "citizenship," is debated by theorists who choose to emphasize one or another of its dimensions. Historically, a lot of emphasis was put on the formal and legal relations between state and individual, as expressed in constitutional and legal procedures of elections and the protection of individual rights. Although these matters are still at the center of many key debates, in the past few decades other aspects of citizenship have received considerable scholarly attention as well. In the 1950s the British sociologist T. H. Marshall defined "social citizenship" as the core of just relations between the state and its members. For him the essence of a just state lies in the allocation of work and welfare opportunities to all members of society.[3] Marshall's depiction of social citizenship as a necessary layer in the commitments of the state to its members is perhaps the most influential deviation from formal conceptualizations of citizenship, and some of its components will resonate in the following discussion. Another contemporary perspective that goes beyond formal relations suggests that solidarity is what amalgamates the complex ties between individual and state.[4]

Unfortunately, few of these discussions relate directly or indirectly to the complexities of democratic citizenship in wartime. Alterations in the popular conceptualization of citizenship, a common social response to war, render most discussions of democratic citizenship less relevant. International conflict, security threats, and a sense of national vulnerability distort the relations of individuals and state, their expectations, their commitments, their rights and obligations. The multilayered relations between individual citizen and democratic state diminish into a narrow relation based on a common interest of endurance.[5] In these circumstances, it is important to reinterpret the relations of individual and state in ways that reflect their changing expectations without abandoning the basic principles that sustain democracy. Let me take a closer look at the changed relations in order to consider which of the reframed aspects requires reiteration and which should be curtailed to preserve democratic values.

Being a Citizen in Times of War

The multidimensional conception of citizenship loses much of its thickness in times of conflict and security threats, and individuals' multiple affiliations to various aspects of society between the family and the state shrink to fit the proclamation "We are all fellow nationals." As an intermediating entity between the private/communal sphere and the state, civil society can represent nationalist sentiments that coincide rather than clash with democratic values and institutions. Simultaneously, the civil society can embody democratic values, sentiments, and behaviors that go hand in hand with the national goals and perspectives as expressed by the nation-state. Most important, civil society can embody the shared fate of compatriots in its complexity.

Wartime generates a set of social processes that can result in reconceptualization of the relations between individual and state, termed here "belligerent citizenship." This conceptualization of citizenship can be described as a return to a crude Hobbesian model of the state, which was established as a way of protecting individuals' lives from the dangers embedded in the "state of nature" and providing them with an opportunity to live more peacefully.[6] The expectations of citizenship in times of war narrow down to resemble this type of relation with the state, in which government can expect much of its citizens in exchange for their protection from violent death. In a different sense, these narrow relations are a reflection of Maslow's hierarchy of needs,[7] according to which, if one's physiological and safety needs (including expectations of survival) are in danger, the urgent requirement to address those needs trumps all others. In war this focus creates a narrower notion of individual-state relations.

Thus, belligerent citizenship emerges as a response to perceived threats to national and personal security. As regarded through this narrow lens, the first responsibility of the state toward its members, as it is quickly reconfigured in the public sphere, is to protect their lives. This responsibility overrides the demand for civil liberties, and those are often steamrolled over by the overpowering sense of urgency to fight for survival.[8] The support of free speech diminishes, both through the criminalization of incitement and through the suppression of deviating opinions via social mechanisms that command unity of voice and subscription to a narrow form of patriotism. Belligerent citizenship is distinctly characterized by a reinterpreted notion of three key components of democratic citizenship, namely, civic participation, unity and solidarity (also known as patriotism), and public deliberation.[9] In times of war these take the form of an emphasis on citizens' contribution to the country rather than on voluntary participation; support for social unity and patriotism over diversity; and consequently, the discouragement of deliberation.[10] In describing these aspects of belligerent citizenship, I point to the contemporary Israeli and American experiences, as characterized both by the media and by scholarly research on the two countries. Pointing out significant differences between the two countries is easy. The differences are presumably due to a number of factors, including the immediacy and persistence of the threat in the Israeli case, the geographic distance of most military operations from U.S. soil, the duration of the conflict, and the greater historical commitment to democracy in the United States. In addition, Israel is unique in mandating universal conscription and decades-long reserve service for most male citizens even in relatively quiet times. Despite these significant differences, similarities can be traced in the responses of both countries to the circumstances of conflict that make the comparison worthwhile. I am not attempting a thorough methodical comparison between the countries, for my aim is more normative than descriptive. The basis of the comparison is the suggestion that both countries, like some other democratic countries in history, are immersed in protracted conflicts. A protracted conflict, with no clear aims and consequently no well-defined attainable mode of achieving victory, casts a different burden on society than other types of war. When Britain and the United States fought against Nazi Germany and its allies in World War II, they did not know when or how the war would end. But the goals were clearly defined, allowing the citizens to assess the acts of their governments and participate in various ways (beyond conscription) in the war effort. The struggle, albeit long, was focused on a clear mission, and although civil society was not invited to participate in all decisions (the nuclear bomb is an easy example, but there are many others), citizens had access to abundant information about the campaign. A protracted conflict, more blurry in goals and modus operandi, creates unique challenges to civil society. I am thus borrowing from the experiences of these two countries to outline some of the most significant social responses to wartime that relate to the evolution of belligerent citizenship.

The focus of civic participation during periods of conflict or security threats shifts from the open and voluntary to the directed and mandated. The measure of civic participation is no longer civic engagement but the readiness to contribute to the war and the survival effort, and possibly to risk one's life for the sake of the country.[11] In Israel where military service is compulsory, volunteering for combat service is considered the utmost civic virtue.[12] The very concept of the "citizen," revered in peaceful times as the cornerstone of democratic practices, is undercut in times of war by its comparison to a more powerful one, namely, "the soldier." The focus of belligerent citizenship on the value of contribution to the war effort makes the citizen second in rank to the soldier, who actively participates in the struggle. The soldier is joined by others who contribute to the security effort or respond to threats: in the United States, firefighters were thus characterized for a while after September 11. In chapter 4 I will suggest that women are often characterized through their traditional gender roles as contributing to the war effort by supporting the fighters. In countries that do not mandate universal conscription, the measures of good citizenship are not derived from active participation (or demonstrated willingness to participate) in the war effort. The expectations of good citizenship are hence related more to compliance and support of the basic needs of society as those are constructed through the lens of security threats. These measures are expressed by patriotic unity and suppressed deliberation.

A second distinctive feature of belligerent citizenship is an overpowering form of patriotic unity. War and perceived threats to national security tend to generate a knee-jerk response of unification. "This is an attack on all Americans," President Bush said in one of his first responses to the September 11 attacks. Three days after the attacks he said, "Our people are together, and we will prevail." A sense of solidarity, unity, and a common cause are regarded by political psychologists as part of the required attitudes for enduring an intractable conflict. "The purpose of beliefs of unity is to provide a sense that all members of the society support the goals of the conflict and their leaders. They act to strengthen the solidarity and stability. . . . [A] lack of unity, on the other hand, creates polarization and internal tensions that hamper the struggle with the enemy."[13] The ensuing solidarity enables recuperation from the distress that conflict (or an attack) creates, for it strengthens the ability to envision a response to the threat, a positive and active outcome beyond the vulnerability it generates.

The solidarity with fellow citizens is intensified when relating to members of the military. The troops, or "our children," as they are often termed in the Israeli public debate, are to be spared any controversy and given full support because they are the manifestation of the national resolve and unity (as well as the nation's actual protectors in many cases). During the Republican National Convention preceding the 2004 election, the keynote speaker, Zell Miller (D-GA), expressed this sentiment with fervor: "Now, while young Americans are dying in the sands of Iraq and the mountains of Afghanistan, our nation is being torn apart and made weaker because of the Democrats' manic obsession to bring down our Commander in Chief."[14] Some commentators did mention that election-year attempts to offer an alternative candidate for the presidency should still be regarded as legitimate, even though the current president is also the commander in chief. But the public debate seemed to be less than tolerant of attacks on the president or on the Bush administration's decisions, and the Democrats restricted their "negative campaigning" accordingly. The demands for patriotic unity thus quelled the democratic process, and not merely because of a cynical exploitation of these patriotic feelings. The demand for national unity seems to be an authentic manifestation of a social need. The political responses to this kind of constraint or requirement may vary, but an approach to citizenship (and civic education) that aims to remain relevant in times of conflict ought to take them into account—not necessarily foster them, but respond to them.

The third feature of belligerent citizenship is the suppression of deliberation and, consequently, an attenuation of the public sphere. Deliberation is far less encouraged in a state of war than in other times, or the ideal that democratic models aspire to. Deliberation and disagreement are widely regarded as threats to the security effort, and the more real and pressing the security threat becomes, the narrower the limits of acceptable perspectives in public debate. In situations of a protracted conflict, the public agenda tends to be focused around security issues, and a vast range of opinions is perceived as unreasonable or irrelevant. Hence, fewer subjects are deemed worthy of public discussion, and fewer perspectives are regarded as deserving representation in the public deliberation.[15]

The attenuation of the public agenda ensues from the extensive attention given to issues surrounding the conflict and generates a diminishing commitment to free speech. Whereas in the United States, economic and other social issues still take a central place in the media and in public discussions along with the "war on terrorism," the public debate in Israel focuses almost exclusively on the armed conflict. However, the news media and the processes of legislation in both countries show significant evidence of declining commitment to free speech in the name of public security. The Patriot Act (officially titled the USA PATRIOT Act) has contributed significantly to this trend,[16] while in Israel numerous incidents have been reported in which newspapers were shut down, news stories censured, and public figures deemed public threats, in the name of security and under the Emergency Regulations that have been in place since the establishment of the state of Israel in 1948. The chief justice of Israel's High Court famously noted that "in a society based on democratic values, human rights can be limited in order to protect human feelings." When the emotional capacity of the public is diminished by the continuous stress of security threats, these "human feelings" become less durable, allowing the public to demand more and more limitations on such "disturbing" rights as freedom of speech and of the press. The public may urge the media to protect its right not to know, not to be intrigued, not to participate.

The most problematic effect from a democratic perspective is not that of formal censorship or narrowing boundaries of free speech (as problematic as those are). The most problematic consequence of the attenuation of the public sphere is self-censorship, the subsiding tolerance in the public for hearing and corresponding with a variety of perspectives, and the silencing effect of this intolerance. The effects of belligerent citizenship on the democratic public sphere become clearer through the examination of some of the social processes evident in the Israeli and American polities.

Unity and Its Discontents: Belligerent Citizenship in the United States and Israel

Israeli citizenship has long been torn between two conceptualizations: liberal citizenship on the one hand and, on the other, a combination of the remnants of republican citizenship associated with the colonial settlement with an ever more religiously defined ethnonationalist citizenship.[17] The latter, which carries a significant similarity to belligerent citizenship, is more likely to take precedence in more acute situations of concern for national security (and consequently for personal safety). The various aspects of belligerent citizenship—the expectation from the government to take more direct responsibility for individual choices and practices, even at the price of losing some rights and liberties; the overpowering sense of patriotic unity; and the narrow focus of the public debate on security issues—push aside those aspects of liberal citizenship that are manifested in quieter times.

The willingness of many citizens to surrender a certain degree of liberty for the sake of acquiring a stronger (sense of) security is evident in the public responses to, among other things, restricted movement for certain groups, roadblocks, and restrictions on free speech in public and via the media. This is also a testament to the limited scope of public debate—what is considered both interesting and important are almost solely matters that directly pertain to personal safety in the context of national security.

Additionally, the perceived existential threat and the uncertain security situation create a tendency in Israeli society to cultivate unity among the Jewish groups within it. The sense of belonging and solidarity is reinforced, and the aspects common to all groups emphasized, under the heading "We are all Jews," in an effort to minimize the gaps between Jews of different ethnicity or religious convictions. One of the societal beliefs that are necessary for a society to stand firm during a protracted conflict is the belief in social unity, which is part of belligerent citizenship.

The sense of unity generates alienation among members of groups that do not feel that they are appropriately represented in the public political discourse. Conversely, the belief in unity naturally induces a sense of common fate, belonging, and closeness. The sense of unity broadly encompasses all the citizens of the state of Israel who are not Palestinians. Situations of existential distress in a security context, particularly terrorist attacks and the constant fear of terrorism, strengthen the sense of unity and dispel tensions between the different groups of Jewish citizens.

Yet the thin veil of unity, which obscures social divisions among the Israeli Jewish public, is also a source of tension, particularly between democratic commitments and the sort of patriotism that fuels the unity. A focus on common enemies and formulations such as "We are all Jews" make it difficult to create a meaningful public space. Members of different groups find that the cultural contents that are relevant to them are not reflected in the public sphere because it is mainly devoted to security issues. Dissimilarities between groups that are in fact valuable, as well as problems of certain groups that need to be dealt with on the social plane, are deferred to "better days."

Thus, social unity (or the belief in such unity), which is augmented when the perceived existential threat worsens, has desirable social effects. On the one hand, it mostly fosters a sense of belonging that is regarded as a positive factor in social relations, in addition to supporting endurance through hard times. On the other hand, it carries problematic consequences—primarily the tendency to sweep divisive issues under the rug.

Eliminating potentially divisive topics from the public agenda is problematic both in the short and in the long run. When the conflict still takes center stage, the effects of disappearing social issues may not be significant. But as time goes by, particularly during protracted conflicts, the issues deemed irrelevant or not urgent enough to warrant social attention in times of war could take a toll on minority groups and on society as a whole.

Moreover, after the end of the conflict, when the need to maintain societal beliefs that enable resilience in the face of threat diminishes, so too will the need for the belief in unity. The neglected social issues could rise into the public sphere with a vengeance. For one, issues may have deteriorated as a result of the lack of social attention, such as welfare matters, minority group standing, or educational disputes. In addition, in some cases the end of conflict could create a split between those who support the peace treaties and those who oppose them. When what is at stake is of genuine importance to the citizens, this could mark the beginning of a new rift between the "winners" and the "losers." Against the backdrop of a decline in the commitment to democracy that characterizes periods of conflict, this situation could be perilous to social cohesion. In Israel there exists a clear potential that intra-Jewish rifts will emerge after peace comes, especially with the ceding of Israeli sovereignty over occupied territories. Without significant public educational efforts, these rifts could put democracy itself under threat.

In post–September 11 America, strong preliminary evidence indicates some similar processes of emerging belligerent citizenship.[18] The American public shares with Israel and other democracies a propensity to "rally 'round the flag" when the country is involved in an international crisis.[19] This phenomenon of surging support for the president and the administration in times of war has been related to various factors, most prominently to a surge in patriotism.[20] As Rogers Smith indicates in an insightful article, when President George W. Bush began his administration, his conception of America's role among nations more closely resembled "the City on the Hill" conception than an interventionist one.[21] The move from a focus on America as a "promised land" to stressing its role as a "crusader state," or even a "benevolent superpower," coincides with the tragic events of September 11. Internally, this move signifies an emergent protector role for the state, which is beneficial to many (from a psycho-political perspective) and detrimental to some, and it includes the potential for weakening democratic commitments if not properly addressed.

In the aftermath of September 11, the social intolerance toward American Muslims grew significantly. One study concluded that after the attacks, Americans were "rallying around each other, concerned and even distrustful of some groups of foreigners. This is a kind of patriotism of mutual support."[22] In addition, the suppression of deviating opinions was clearly seen in the

American public sphere after September 11. Support for the president surged,[23] and various venues of public debate grew reluctant to criticize the administration's decisions.[24] The new or renewed sense of patriotism, solidarity, and unity, which some cherished as a positive "change of heart,"[25] could also account for a diminished support for free speech, for the reluctance to condemn the loss of civil liberties, and for the low-key public deliberation over the aims and means of the war waged on terror in its first stages.[26]

Some evidence for valuing patriotic unity over free speech could be found in the academic world. In January 2003, the University of California at Berkeley refused to allow a fund-raising appeal for the Emma Goldman Papers Project because the appeal quoted Goldman on the suppression of free speech and her opposition to war (writing during World War I, before she was deported to Russia).[27] Even before the war in Iraq began, the winds of war created much caution on various educational forums: "After complaints that the children of soldiers were upset by anti-war comments at school, Maine's top education official warned teachers to be careful of what they say in class about a possible invasion of Iraq."[28]

The criticism of the war in Iraq intensified as the war turned into a protracted conflict and as it became apparent that the reasons the administration offered the public for going to war were faulty, and that the preparation for the phase of "winning the peace" or nation-building was lacking at best. The fairly unified public sphere turned more divided as the 2004 election neared. However, its narrowed limits remained as such, with security issues dominating both presidential campaigns and the public discourse at large, and with the scope of what could be said about the war, its justification, and its aims still limited. The lives lost made it hard for public figures to express opposition to the war, reflecting the tendency even when opposing the war to stay within the limits of unified patriotism.

This phenomenon is by no means new. In democratic countries, where patriotism is considered to be freely expressed rather than orchestrated by the authorities, wartime promotes a surge in expressions of national sentiments. Such surges, among others, were described in the United States during World War II and the cold war,[29] in Britain during World War II,[30] in Canada during World War I,[31] and during various eras of conflict in France.[32] The loosely defined "war on terrorism" in which the United States is involved, and the ongoing conflict Israel has endured for most of the half century since it was established, are similar in their effect on patriotic sentiments.

The drawbacks of the belligerent form of citizenship can be further illustrated through the Israeli version of national unity. A closer look reveals that we are not really "all Jews." Some— over 18 percent—are Muslim and Christian Palestinians; others are of a variety of denominations and national origins. Not all Israeli citizens share the burdens of military service; hence, not all have a chance to be considered good citizens. Israeli belligerent citizenship marginalizes groups that are exempt from military service—such as most Palestinian citizens, religiously observant women, and disabled youth. Conscientious objectors are widely considered beyond the pale of acceptable public discourse and action.

The sense of national unity and solidarity withstands all of these exclusions and maintains such a strong place in the public ethos and debate that it can effectively curtail the claims of excluded groups. The concept of unity functions as a very simple control mechanism over the public debate, as expressed by Andrew Arato in an article highly critical of the Bush administration after September 11: "If he wins this fight, we win. If he loses it, we lose."[33]

Thus, the main challenge facing democratic theories of citizenship in times of war is the diminishing scope of the public agenda, which tends to be overtaken by security issues and is tolerant of a narrowing range of opinions on these topics. Thus, for example, deliberative models significantly rely upon a presupposition of substantive diversity of opinion. If all or most citizens express the same preferences, the deliberative process loses much of its appeal, as it "associates democracy with open discussion and the exchange of views leading to agreed-upon policies."[34] It relies on the assumptions that the polity offers an open public space, proper means of communication as well as the motivation to communicate, an acceptable range of opinions, and a variety of issues on which to deliberate. "Democratic process,"

Iris Marion Young reminds us, "is primarily a discussion of problems, conflicts, and claims of need or interest."[35] For Amy Gutmann and Dennis Thompson, the process of deliberation embodies not only procedural but also principled aspects.[36] The model of deliberative democracy is hence based on an assumption of a variety of topics and a vast array of opinions, constrained by democratic values, as background conditions for the successful practice of democracy. When faced with overwhelming agreement, the purpose of deliberation and its value diminish.

In sum, belligerent citizenship is advantageous for a society in times of war because it helps the citizens survive the hard times and respond to them constructively. It fosters a mutual sense of belonging and supports endurance during hard times. However, it comes at a high cost. First, this unity is thin, elusive, and exclusionary, and therefore cultivates intolerance toward various subgroups. It alienates members of groups that are not properly represented in the public political discourse. This cost is borne mainly by minorities, who are either excluded from the national solidarity or refuse to participate in its rites of patriotism. It is also borne by democracy itself. Moreover, this type of social unity and solidarity comes at the cost of political stagnation—an inability to envision and support change in the political circumstances. This stagnation is partly a result of a narrowed public sphere and a public agenda that is so rigorously devoted to security issues that it tends to neglect or postpone other social matters, and partly it is a consequence of the suppression of dissenting perspectives.

When democratic commitments are suppressed by the public's response to perceived threats, there is a growing risk that the democratic ideal will become subordinate to the survival of the state. Belligerent citizenship is not dichotomously distinct from democratic citizenship. The move from one to the other does not happen overnight. Rather it is a gradual closing of options, an uneven process of narrowing down perceptions—a slippery slope, if you will, from the wide-open democratic entrance to the funnel, to its authoritarian closed end.

Hence, wartime creates a special need to protect democratic commitments in a contextual way, responding to the unique social circumstances of war. It creates a greater need to foster and enhance civic relations among members of the nation, to expand

21

the public agenda, to encourage participation and engagement, and to support an inclusive conception of citizenship. The ways in which civil society and the education system perceive citizenship can affect their ability to endorse these commitments.

The most relevant theoretical tool for the purpose of responding to these challenges can be found in democratic theories that discuss citizenship in relation to notions of nationalism and patriotism.[37] These theories suggest that debates about citizenship are, in essence, debates about nationhood and what it means to belong to a national group.[38] Looking at citizenship through the lens of nationalism and patriotism can help to unfold the layers of expectations citizens and the state have for each other. The analysis of these expectations, informed by democratic (and sometimes liberal-democratic) ideals, reveals the desirable—or at least unthreatening—aspects of citizenship as *amore di patria*. As a preliminary illustration, consider Yael Tamir's suggestion that the concept "citizenship" creates a link between liberalism and nationality. For her, the nation-state is a community, and as such it can require its members to show general civic competence as well as "a competence to act as a member of *this* particular community."[39] Only through the notion of nationalism as communal identity can political associations be understood as a liberal endeavor, she claims. Hence, a further aspect beyond democratic commitments enters the complex picture of citizenship: belonging to a particular national group, with its unique culture, norms, and history. Understanding citizenship as related to membership in a national group is an essential prelude to considering the more problematic aspects of patriotism as the essence of belligerent citizenship. A positive formulation of patriotic citizenship can contribute to the main aim of this book, namely, exploring possible ways of constructively responding to the challenges that wartime poses for the project of civic education. However, this positive notion of national citizenship is often constructed as an identity-related project. A closer look at the relations between nationalism, patriotism, and citizenship is thus needed here, along with a critique of the conceptualization of citizenship as identity.

CITIZENSHIP AS SHARED FATE (OR DOOM)

Most conceptions of democratic citizenship regard it—directly or by implication—as an aspect of individual and collective identity. This conceptualization produces a few educational drawbacks; before exploring these I will focus on the problematic social consequences of conceptualizing citizenship as a given aspect of individual and group identity. To support democratic inclinations, democratic citizenship should be perceived not only as an aspect of identity but also as shared fate. This alternative concept is more productive and offers a better understanding of the civic challenges democratic societies face both in times of peace and during war. Understanding citizenship as shared fate rather than solely as an identity-related matter can offer a proper basis for understanding belligerent citizenship and for developing a democratic educational response to its challenges.

The formulation of citizenship as identity stems from the notion that it is membership-based, founded on an alliance of an individual with a nation-state. Acquiring citizenship in a nation-state is commonly based on either birthright or formal processes of naturalization, which in turn requires a manifestation of certain forms of worthiness. For various ends, most notably nation-building, affective attachments to the regime and to fellow citizens serve as fundamental prerequisites.[40] Regarding oneself as a member of the nation by identity, and not only by virtue of interest or choice, is conducive to political cooperation among members of the national community. It can support the processes of choosing ends and pursuing them, of constructing a public agenda and deliberating its fulfillment. Additionally, it can enhance mutual cultural (and other communal) practices that maintain justice and a sense of belonging. Eamonn Callan regards the emotional attachment of citizens to each other as a basis for liberal patriotism, which is a condition for liberal justice (and which he claims makes a case for teaching certain forms of patriotism in public schools).[41] In the same vein, Tamir argues that "[s]ince the roots of unity in national communities are outside the normative sphere, they can accommodate normative diversity" and support a pluralistic public sphere.[42] For these and other liberal authors, conceiving of nationalism as identity is a way of endorsing pluralism, which is maintained even through times of conflict. The pluralism that this notion of citizenship supposedly contains parallels the diversity that a number of other theorists regard as part and parcel of the communal relations that are based on "identity citizenship." Both share an assumption—an unwarranted one, as I suggest—that ethnic, religious, and ideological diversity make up the civil society, and that those features can be accommodated and tolerated through the shared notion of national identity.

Regarding citizenship as a form of identity requires an assumption, as well as a political insistence, that diversity "is kept in its place," in Stephen Macedo's words.[43] Many theorists are concerned mostly with the *containment* of diversity within the polity. For them the definition of citizenship as a form of identity is a helpful response to possible challenges from individuals' affiliation with other subgroups (or supranational groups). The main threat they identify to the desirable forms of civic affiliation and liberal nationalism is diversity, or competing commitments to groups other than the nation. Although individuals are assumed to possess a multiplicity of identities, their national identity is expected by most liberals theorists to trump, ideally, conflicting demands from other identities with which they associate themselves. The affective attachment to fellow citizens, for example, should serve as a barrier to the demands of secession by subgroups within the nation-state. National identity in its desirable liberal form—admittedly not the only form generated by national attachments throughout history—supersedes other forms of identity, to the extent that the various groups and individuals that make up the regime all regard themselves as integral and willing parts in it.

Contrary to this suggestion, in times of war ideological diversity diminishes, and with it tolerance to other forms of diversity. Conceiving of citizenship as an aspect of identity—and inculcating this form of citizenship through state institutions such as the public education system—threatens to further escalate these expressions of belligerent citizenship. In order to preclude the less desirable forms of nationalism including those expressed though belligerent citizenship, some form of diversity is preferable. One of the unique challenges that wartime presents to civic society is the overarching consensus on civic affiliations, national goals, and proper perspectives. This form of unity supplants diversity and thus creates a new challenge—the need to support and encourage diversity rather than merely contain its existing forms.

When belligerent citizenship evolves, diversity is suppressed for the perceived sake of national survival, generating a need to rethink the conceptualization of citizenship as identity. When citizenship is conceptualized as a source of personal identity, the threat to the nation is more easily conceived of as a personal and existential threat. Moreover, the sense of personal attachment that is the basis of identity citizenship intensifies in times of conflict. If citizens conceive of their membership in the political community mainly as an identity matter, they are less likely to find ways of mitigating the less democratic effects of belligerent citizenship. Even in times of a controversial conflict, when large parts of society do not subscribe to the patriotic unity expected in times of war or fail to join the rally 'round the flag, patriotism is stressed in the public debate more forcefully. The role of the dissenting parties is to prove themselves still entitled to be fellow nationals, and they face an ongoing struggle not to be described as "beyond the pale." Even civic society, heralded by some theorists as a barrier to monolithic, oppressive perceptions of the nation that the government, absent civic institutions, could inculcate, does not always support or maintain diversity in times of conflict.[44] To the contrary, civic institutions may partake in the processes that reflect and promote the narrow, unifying, and exclusive conceptualizations of national group membership.

Most theorists regard the conceptualization of citizenship as identity not solely as a descriptive project but rather as an educational endeavor. Therefore, it is important to note the normative inadequacies of this undertaking, particularly as they are exacerbated in times of conflict. Inculcating civic affiliations in the form of identity through the public school's civic curriculum could unwittingly harm the causes of civic nationalism. Callan, Tamir, Gutmann, Macedo, and many others share an affinity with civic and democratic commitments, and they all believe—as do I—that these commitments should be promoted through the public school system (although they do not all agree on the

25

specifics of the methods and contents). But these causes can be advanced in schools only if diversity is "kept in its place" not only against rising tides of communal claims, secessionist demands, and manifestations of "politics of difference," as these theorists suggest. They must also be maintained against the stifling effects of mandated national solidarity. Working to preserve rather than contain diversity is an educational aim that can better be met through teaching citizenship as a form of shared fate rather than through presenting citizenship solely as identity.

Melissa Williams suggests that the portrayal of citizenship as part of individuals' personal identity has a number of further relevant deficiencies.[45] She argues convincingly that citizenship as identity can hardly be reconciled with "the egalitarian treatment of citizens from cultural and religious minorities."[46] In circumstances of suppressed diversity and diminished trust, this deficiency can grow into a significant threat to democratic attitudes. This is even more troublesome when coupled with Williams's other point of criticism against the major role given to loyalty in this context. Readily admitting that "a loyal citizenry can contribute to political stability in ways that are fully consonant with democratic equality," she raises the concern that "the valorization of citizen loyalty as a virtue" should be regarded more suspiciously. "The dark side of the claim that we have good reason to trust fellow citizens who affirm their [civic and national] commitment . . . is the implication that we have good reason to *distrust* individuals who refuse to affirm this commitment."[47] Clearly this dark side grows darker when citizens are more easily inclined to distrust individuals and groups within the nation, and when they define their trust in narrow patriotic terms. In circumstances of conflict, the distrustful responses to certain ethnic and religious minorities (such as the responses to Arab Americans after September 11) grow more evident and more violent. Using loyalty and mutual trust as the basis of citizenship (when perceived as identity) generates the immediate risk of blaming "others" for being disloyal or untrustworthy. Wartime creates a demand for unconditional loyalty and "treats everything short of such loyalty as an act of unforgivable treason."[48] The stress and uncertainty of a protracted conflict make such responses more readily available to citizens who were

26

raised to regard themselves as Americans by identity, and to trust those (or only those) who identify themselves similarly to a satisfactory level.[49]

Moreover, the promise of political stability that is supposed to stem from the concept of citizenship as identity can turn sour in times of war. Political stability, often a desirable factor,[50] can signify in times of war an unwillingness or inability to support change. Stability can easily turn into rigidity, or stagnation, when the notion of citizenship narrows down to a demand to identify with a common perception of national goals, and to contribute to the cause of national survival. Hence, citizenship as identity can be problematic from the liberal perspective as well as other democratic perspectives in peaceful times, and more significantly so in times of war.

An alternative understanding of citizenship is based not on interpretations of identity but rather on ties among the members of the community and the mutual effects of their political choices. Democratic societies are better served by a public and educational focus on what the citizenry shares as related to individuals' fate rather than to their personal and communal identity. Members in a democratic society share a commitment to the social contract that unites them; they share a voice in the choice of representatives and in those representatives being held accountable to them as a citizenry. They share access to public institutions and a commitment to (at least) some basic symbols of their national group as expressed in the democratic processes and the basic structure of their society. Conceiving of national affiliation as an aspect of identity marginalizes these issues while focusing on what is conceptualized as "essential," namely, those matters that are derivative of nationalism as identity. Conceptualizing citizenship as shared fate offers a more persuasive understanding of citizenship as well as a more promising educational endeavor. Citizenship as shared fate can be based on a shared cultural identity (much like citizenship as identity), but it can also be based on many other features, among them institutional linkages (such as a representative government), material linkages, and "seeing our own narratives as entwined with those of others."[51] In a broader discussion, Rogers Smith examines a similar descriptive and educational endeavor of constituting citizenship based on historical perceptions rather than naturalistic ones.[52] Naturalistic understandings of citizenship are easily equated with conceptualizations of citizenship as identity, in particular in cases in which this identity is portrayed as given rather than as a historical notion that can be revised, criticized, reinterpreted, and amended by the individuals and groups that make up the national community. The historical understanding of national affiliation transforms citizens' conception of themselves as belonging to a group, and helps them own it in a more active way, as they see themselves as individuals (or members of specific groups within the nation) who are responsible for the reinterpretation of their national group over time. This understanding also supports deliberative aims.

The conceptualization of citizenship as shared fate, or as a historical rather than a natural endeavor, is echoed in contemporary discussions on citizenship. Some of the recent writings on multiculturalism and citizenship rely to some extent on this notion. The suggestion that the institutional linkage creates a unique obligation or associative duty to our compatriots can be traced to the claim for prioritizing the interests of our fellow citizens because our political choices will result in laws that they too must obey. More broadly, the officials we elect together will implement policies that influence all of our lives, whether we voted for them or not. Therefore, the shared fate can be partially described as part of the aggregative model of citizenship, based, as an educational endeavor, on an argument from mutual effect.

In addition, economic factors play an important role in describing citizenship as shared fate. From Ernest Gellner's historical analysis of nationalism as an economic project,[53] to more recent discussions of local and global environmental effects, the resources we share with our fellow citizens are a fundamental part of what unites us.

In the conceptual realm, Williams's suggestion that the narratives that we share with others are what turn us into compatriots in the fuller sense is close in spirit to Anderson's description of an imagined community. "Having a sense of ourselves as members of a community of fate entails telling ourselves (true) stories about how we came to be connected," she writes,[54] echoing Anderson's contention that the imagined community is what turns a group of unaffiliated individuals into a nation.

Some interpret the shared fate argument as having a communitarian strike, a suggestion that raises a host of criticisms directed against this trend of thought. The heart of the critical argument against shared fate is expressed in Dana Villa's claim that the "encumbered self" represented in this approach should be viewed as the exemplar of the unexamined life, and thus should be rejected as the root of personal immorality and social injustice. For him, any group affiliation, and the reliance on conventional thought that ensues from belonging to a group and appreciating its traditions, stands in the way of critical thought and thus is opposed to the ideal of philosophical citizenship (or the idea that one should express her civic affiliation through the political questioning of her society's beliefs, traditions, and mores). For Villa, the cultivation of shared affiliation is what induces "moral slumber," the source of uncritical and thus unjust state of affairs in society.[55]

Note that although the argument here supports the communal affiliation expressed in citizenship as shared fate, it converges more closely with Villa's constructive suggestion than with the communitarian approaches he criticizes. Citizenship as shared fate does not describe social membership as "evident" but rather as an individual and communal interpretative project that is a central aspect of civic life. The objective of this process is not the unquestioning endorsement of one's nationality. To the contrary, it is the understanding of the open, flexible, and contingent nature of national and communal affiliation as a shared project. Social life, communal perceptions, and the understanding of oneself as a citizen are all contingent upon the constant construction and reinterpretation of the shared aspects. It is thus a calling not for a blind acceptance of historical "facts" or myths, or of membership as a pillar of one's identity. Rather it is the demand for an active participation in the construction of a historic community that is not constrained by a final vision of the good social life or the common good. True, those conceptions would be affected by social circumstances, and it is possible that they will tend to become less tolerant or less critical in times of conflict. The cure for that, however, cannot be trusted

29

on the appearance of a Socratic "gadfly" who would wake the nation from its dogmatic slumber (as Villa seems to suggest). Rather, the cure must be the continual, institutional commitment to diversity, debate, and challenges to "evident" views. This aim can most significantly be supported by a civic education committed to active engagement and participation in the construction of national affiliation as shared fate.

Conceptualizing citizenship as membership in a community of shared fate carries some valuable implications. Most notably it supports an ahierarchical notion of community, as all can participate in its construction, a thin layer of identity that promotes trust among a wide variety of subgroups, and practical reciprocity in the continual process of shaping the meaning and implication of membership. Those implications are beneficial in any period of a nation's existence; along with others, they can be proven crucial in times of war, in their ability to offset the undemocratic consequences of belligerent citizenship. First, "the idea of citizenship as shared fate does not presuppose that all individuals' or groups' understandings of their place . . . need to be the same as those of all others."[56] Espousing a communal structure that is open to various interpretations can support and validate an open-minded response to a vast variety of conceptions about the community. Fostering shared deliberation, skills of critical reasoning, and reflection are all civic virtues that arise from conceiving citizenship as shared fate, and all of them are potential reinforcements to democracy in times of war.

Conceiving of citizenship as shared fate is thus a productive addition to its conceptualization as identity, in peaceful times and even more so in times of conflict. But in order for it to provide a substantive response to belligerent citizenship, we need to consider some further aspects of this notion, most prominently the suggestion that "good citizenship is something we know from individuals' *acts* rather than from their *beliefs*."[57] This suggestion is aimed at countering the emphasis of "citizenship as identity" notions of loyalty as a set of emotions, positions, and beliefs, and the dangers that this emphasis poses to democratic liberties. That individuals develop a perception of themselves as participants in a shared project, judged by their acts rather than by their beliefs, is Williams's cure for this difficulty.

But employing this notion of citizenship as shared fate to socie-ties in times of war, in the service of countering belligerent citi-zenship, creates a new difficulty. Because belligerent civic con-ceptions are based on a narrow set of possible acts of loyalty, namely, acts that contribute to national survival, this aspect of citizenship as shared fate can be proven obstructive to the aim of preserving democracy in wartime. In other words, if we judge civic loyalty through an individual's acts, we may not face the privacy and liberty issues that arise from judging loyalty based on one's beliefs, but we may face further issues of excluding those members who fail—or refuse—to act according to consen-sual demands for action. For example, if in Israel citizenship pre-scribes active military service as proof of one's loyalty and as an entry card to the national mainstream, disabled citizens who are not conscripted may be left outside the realm of good citizen-ship. At least as disturbing is the fact that the acts of those who oppose the political-military endeavors in the occupied territo-ries and declare themselves selective conscientious objectors are considered manifestations of withdrawal from the domain of Is-raeli citizenship. The Israeli example can be generalized to other democracies in conflict, in which those who do not demonstra-tively participate in the strict rites of good belligerent citizenship are regarded suspiciously by their fellow nationals.

Hence, in order to implement the notion of citizenship as shared fate to the context of a democracy at war, particularly to serve as the basis of an educational project, it needs to be adapted to circumstances whereby the shared fate turns into a perceived shared doom. The inculcation of democratic civic commitment through public institutions, most notably the pub-lic education system, is the first and foremost path to main-taining desirable notions of citizenship in society. But considered against the background of belligerent citizenship, societies fac-ing a protracted conflict should devote more attention to pre-serving democracy than they usually do, through civic educa-tion and other means. Belligerent citizenship creates a unique set of challenges to democracies, among them a growing sense of patriotic unity, a growing support for security measures even when they conflict with civil liberties, and a reduced tendency for deliberation. To counter these tendencies without ignoring the emotions that inform them, some form of merging the notions of citizenship as identity and citizenship as shared fate would be helpful. A proper response to belligerent citizenship would be based on an endorsement of beliefs related to membership in the group, along with various acts that express and construct communal shared fate. In other words, although there is room for far more emphasis on the shared destiny of members along with stressing the importance of critical appraisal, alternative narration, or multiple perspectives on what constitutes this fate, it is crucial to acknowledge at the same time the moral reality of many individuals' perception of themselves as members of a nation by identity. This acknowledgment, mitigated by the notion of shared fate, is the basis of the educational endeavor termed here "expansive education." It is based on the sense that the moral realities of belligerent citizenship deserve the attention of scholars and policy makers committed to democracy. Such attention could help support the preservation of democracy, through the continuing process of amending the conceptualization of citizenship. This process is necessitated by the critical endorsement of those aspects of belligerent citizenship that support endurance without threatening democratic values. Various public institutions should partake in the effort to preserve democracy in times of war—elected officials, the courts, and the media all share the responsibility of balancing the needs of a society in conflict with the enduring requirements of a democratic polity. I choose to focus on the role of the public education system in preserving democracy in times of conflict because it is the one public institution that can most effectively foster the positive aspects of the social responses to war while cultivating the necessary attitudes and capacities to challenge the destructive ones and to preserve democracy. I consider the challenges that this system faces in the next chapter and build upon them a constructive response to belligerent citizenship throughout the remainder of the book.

Education as War by Other Means

> Long range values . . . must be subordinated
> to the life-and-death needs of today and
> tomorrow.
> —Education Policies Commission, *What the
> Schools Should Teach in Wartime* (Washington,
> DC, 1943)

THIS CHAPTER EXPLORES the ways in which the public education system conforms to the opening quote. The social and administrative expectation to position security concerns as an educational priority manifests an important way in which belligerent citizenship is reflected in the public education system. Before exploring normatively desirable means for the education system to cope with war and belligerent citizenship, this chapter portrays some common responses of the public education system to the circumstances of conflict. The method employed here is not aimed at presenting temporal or spatial systematic descriptions, because this is meant to be an applied philosophical argument, not a sociological or historical work. It does not attempt to explore one specific era in the life of one nation, or to describe developments in the responses of one nation to various conflicts (although these are worthy aims, and works by others who have undertaken them inform what follows). Rather it illustrates the suggestion that teachers and administrators tend to conform to the mainstream response to war as described in the previous chapter in the discussion of belligerent citizenship. This conformity is described here as harmful to democratic education purposes. The public education system tends to provide the public with what is commonly viewed as the immediate needs of society in times of war. Consequently, it waives various aspects of democratic and civic education, of critical thought and related topics. This seems to be a fundamental flaw, contributing more to the war system than to the interests of society. When the education system is conscripted to teaching belligerent citizenship, it turns education into a part of the war culture; through facilitating the acquisition of belligerent rather than democratic perspectives, education becomes war by other means.

Note that although the educational effects of belligerent citizenship that will be portrayed here constitute an unsettling consequence of wartime, they are not in fact a necessary part of the argument put forth in this book. In other words, the uses of education as "war by other means" are examined only to further exemplify some aspects of the social responses to war or belligerent citizenship. However, the constructive argument presented in this book, namely, that the education system should focus its attention on responding to belligerent citizenship by strengthening democratic commitments through expansive education, does not rely on the actual effects of war on public education. Even if the circumstances of a protracted conflict had no perceptible effect on the common practices of education, the social components of belligerent citizenship and their withering effect on democratic commitments would require an educational response aimed at preserving democracy. Psychologists and educational researchers around the world, working with a host of tools over long periods of time, have noted the significant effects of living through conflict on children's and adolescents' perspectives on war and peace.[1] Learning the relevant conceptualization of war and conflict is a readily available cognitive and emotional process; learning peace and its underlying structures is harder and requires maturity and further investment. In addition, the research provides evidence for the intuition that the more immediate the war experience is to children, the more concrete the related concepts become. Simultaneously, peace becomes more of an abstraction or a simple negation of war. Investing in learning peace could take place only in the public education system, as a public institution whose main justification for using public funds is the preservation of democracy through civic education. This system is the most appropriate one to respond to the changing notions of citizenship through normative responses, such as the one dubbed here "expansive education." As I stressed above, the normative responses to belligerent citizenship are based on working with or responding to it rather than simply opposing it, because belligerent citizenship is a moral reality that cannot be theorized away. In addition it has a positive impact and thus should not be reduced to a threat to democracy. Belligerent citizenship is potentially supportive of stability and endurance, and can provide productive responses to social concerns in times of war. However, it still creates a risk of political stagnation and a diminished form of democratic commitment. Hence, the public education system should work with the changing notions of citizenship to provide future generations of citizens with the tools to appreciate and preserve democracy, as well as plan and prepare for peace, while enduring war. These tools can prove beneficial when citizens face other threats to democracy as well. Whatever the actual responses of the public education system to war may be, public education should develop tools to respond to belligerent citizenship. The discussion in this chapter is thus an illustration of the effects of belligerent citizenship on public education. It portrays some of the challenges to implementing expansive education while stressing the vitality of the normative principles that inform this approach for a democracy at war.

The chapter begins by demonstrating how the belligerent conceptualization of citizenship enhances uncritical nationalistic tendencies in civic education. This claim will be illustrated through Israeli and American public education systems' responses to current respective conflicts. The illustration points to the centrality of patriotic education in creating citizens in wartime. This focal point of belligerent citizenship is situated in the context of the contemporary debate on teaching patriotism. Various arguments in educational and political theory for and against certain versions of patriotic education are weighed, with the conclusion that a nuanced version of patriotic education is required to endure war while defending democracy. This version is based on an understanding of citizenship and national affiliation not solely as an aspect of essential individual identity, but rather as primarily a form of shared fate; consequently, an endorsement of patriotic teaching of history and civics should include an emphasis on democratic values alongside communal affiliation.

35

The Making of (Belligerent) Citizens

In better and worse times, education is the political mechanism by which the state and society shape their future character. Formal educational institutions share with other private and public mechanisms the task of forming the next generation of functioning and contributing citizens. Decision making about the structure of the education system, the curriculum, and, ultimately, the vision that this system will promote, all require consideration of how one wants future society to be shaped. The components of good citizenship vary from one society to the next, from one generation to the next. Changes in economic circumstances, in patterns of inclusion and exclusion, along with the perceived sense of national stability, security, or threat, all influence the ways in which individuals and institutions define desirable modes of citizenship. The education system, as an all-inclusive public institution, carries high social expectations to ensure good citizenship in the next generation.

Within public education systems, civic education is viewed by educational and political theorists as the institutional tool legitimately used to enhance the civic commitments of future citizens. In peaceful times schools commonly aim to balance the teaching of three aspects of social membership. First, democratic processes, civic duties, and rights are taught, consisting of understanding the political system of the state and the roles and liberties of the individual within it. This is the formal aspect of civic education, and it will be not discussed here extensively because it is widely agreed that it forms the necessary (though I suggest insufficient) basis for civic studies.[2] Second, patriotic sentiments are introduced and cultivated, emphasizing national membership and commitments to fellow nationals. These sentiments are learned through formal curricula such as history and literature studies, and through other activities and symbols such as the Pledge of Allegiance, the flag, and the celebration of holidays. This aspect of civic education is explored in detail below in the section on patriotic education. And third, democratic commitments, values, and norms are introduced. This last aspect requires more attention in democracies engaged in a protracted conflict.

In countries where the democratic culture is deeply embedded in the self-perception of the nation, combining and balancing these three aspects of civic education is relatively simple. Some theorists claim that this is one of the public educational advantages of a constitution—this legal and symbolic document upholds democratic principles and values in ways that interweave them with the basic tenets of membership in the nation. It forms part of the educational process in the United States, where democratic norms are commonly introduced through the study of the Constitution, which is part of what defines American public culture. In this way the national character, so to speak, is intertwined with democratic values. In other countries that have no constitution, most notably Britain, the national commitment to democracy is built into the curriculum in other, though no less effective, ways. However, in countries where the relation between national identity and democratic commitment is less obvious, as in Israel (with its inherent tension between Jewish and democratic statehood), the challenges to the education system would be weightier even in peaceful times. Wartime complicates the situation in all those cases.

The outbreak of war often marks an immediate outpouring of patriotic sentiments in democratic countries, where such responses cannot be said to be orchestrated or coerced. "When wars break out," writes Theda Skocpol, "and especially when the nation is attacked, millions of Americans become aware of their *shared identity* and are willing to work together on local and national responses to the crisis."[3] With the first signs of threat, the public opinion tends to extend its support for the government and the education system tends to follow suit. Skocpol assumes in passing that this response is derivative of the conceptualization of citizenship as shared identity. This conceptualization generates some of the more problematic aspects of belligerent citizenship. It has significant problematic effects on the education system's responses to war as well.

How does the education system practically respond to belligerent citizenship? The common response in the Israeli education system is to uncritically reflect the alleged national solidarity and to teach the belligerent form of citizenship through the history and civic studies curricula, the celebration of holidays, and other methods. Many, though not all, of the responses of the

American public sphere and public education system to September 11 point in a similar direction.[4] In past conflicts the American education system's tendency was to reflect the civil society's perspective and therefore to educate for a "unifying" version of patriotism. Cecilia O'Leary shows how the unification of the American public and the mobilization of the nation's youth became possible through the public education system in the latter part of the nineteenth century. Following a struggle between inclusion and "martial patriotism," the latter, belligerent form got the upper hand in the early twentieth century. Consequently, the government "criminalized political dissent, segregated black soldiers, and demonized immigrant Americans unwilling to renounce dual allegiances."[5] The result was a "racially exclusive, culturally conformist, militaristic patriotism [that] finally triumphed over more progressive, egalitarian visions of the nation."[6] O'Leary describes this development as part of a cycle in the conceptualization of American citizenship, which periodically moves between the two visions.

This cycle is influenced by various historical developments, war not the least among them. In wartime students are often presented with a narrow conception of civic virtue, most notably within the less formal aspects of their schooling, through the hidden curriculum or extracurricular activities and—with time—through the curriculum itself as well. Textbooks take a while to catch up with the public expectations, but as the Israeli case demonstrates, they too can grow in time to reflect the demand for a unified, narrow form of patriotism.

In the United States, World War II prompted the creation of the Victory Corps, which was responsible for providing preinduction education to high school youth before they graduated. The Educational Policies Commission of the National Education Association proclaimed that "the war must profoundly modify the entire program of secondary education. . . . [N]o able-bodied boy should graduate from high school in wartime without specific pre-induction training."[7] In an article examining the changes in secondary schools during this era, Richard Ugland notes that "both vocational and academic subjects conformed to the times" by adapting their curricula to respond to wartime requirements. This was not, as he maintains, a good time for liberal education.[8]

Civic education and patriotism are not the sole educational fields affected by the changing social perceptions in times of conflict. During the cold war, science education curricula in the United States underwent vast reforms arising from the contention that the nation had to face *Sputnik*, the galvanizing image of Soviet scientific and technological superiority, in the classroom.[9] In Israel one can find an abundance of references to the nation's need to preserve its "qualitative advantage" over its enemies through education, including vocational education that pertains to military professions. In Britain during World War I, "schools sought to inculcate attitudes that would strengthen national resolve and to intensify activities contributing materially to the war effort."[10]

Such examples can be found in contemporary American schools as much as they are found in historical depictions of responses to past conflicts. In October 2001, the Nebraska state board of education voted unanimously to endorse a 1949 state law that required schools to teach lyrics to patriotic songs, reverence for the flag, and the dangers of communism. Officials at an elementary school in Rocklin, California, declined to remove a God Bless America sign after the American Civil Liberties Union complained that it violated the separation of church and state. Meanwhile, the U.S. House of Representatives gave its blessing to God Bless America, urging public schools to display the expression as a show of support for the nation. The nonbinding resolution passed, 404–0.

These decisions tend to take place without a significant public debate and often constitute an uncritical response to the changes in social conceptualizations of the needs arising from the state of emergency. They may constitute first steps in the problematic direction that the Israeli education system has been taking for decades. A closer look at some of the Israeli responses to the circumstances of conflict and their consequent social demands suggests that educational responses should be of concern to citizens committed to democracy.

How to Replicate War: An Israeli Illustration

In the political and security situation Israel has experienced through most of its existence, the Israeli notion of how schools should prepare the next generation for good citizenship has centered considerably on the components of belligerent citizenship. Those components include preparation for military service, related patriotic moral and social attitudes, and cultivating the beliefs needed to cope with conflict as civilians. In a comprehensive study, Daniel Bar-Tal, an Israeli political psychologist, analyzes a set of required traits and portrays the curriculum as one that aims at cultivating these traits throughout the schooling years.[11] The protracted conflict in which Israel is engaged requires that the citizens develop skills for living with an ongoing existential threat. Bar-Tal asserts that "a society involved in an uncontrolled conflict must develop beliefs that will help it cope successfully with the situation." Among the necessary psychological conditions he enumerates are "dedication to the society and the country, high motivation to contribute, perseverance, coping with physical and psychological pressure, willingness for personal sacrifice, unity, solidarity, upholding the goals of the society, determination, courage and endurance."[12] These conditions clearly correspond with belligerent citizenship and are indeed the psycho-political expressions of this conceptualization of citizenship to which the education system responds.

Beyond the cultivation of these communal affiliations, the Israeli education system responds to actual and perceived security needs by stressing attitudes considered vital for national survival. First among these needs is citizens' willingness to take part in the military effort. The cooperation between the military and the education system consists of Gadna (premilitary) service, which all (non-Orthodox) Jewish high school students are required to perform. Another, less conspicuous, curricular aspect of belligerent civic education relates to the ways in which the Jewish holidays are taught. The holidays, which are an important part of the curriculum for the younger ages, serve as a tool for transmitting a national message of a people perpetually at war and celebrating time after time their victory over Greeks,

Romans, and other enemies throughout history. An emphasis is put on the military aspects that pertain to many Jewish holidays rather than, for example, on universal humanist elements within them.

Geography studies are geared to forming a notion of Israel as part of the Western world and in particular as part of the Mediterranean Basin, an approach that turns its back to the Middle East and the more immediate neighboring countries. History studies emphasize the military history of the state of Israel and the larger story of the persecuted Jewish people while projecting a uniform and uncritical image of the people and state. The Israeli education system chooses to reflect a military-national conception that regards citizenship in the state of Israel as part of a historical struggle for survival. Membership in the nation is correspondingly conceived of as part of a (Jewish) religious historical and cultural identity, fused through decades of struggle. This educational interpretation is a systemic response to the mainstream conceptualization of citizenship, in line with the sociopsychological needs of people in times of conflict. The prevalence of this response is evident on occasion in the highest level of government: in August 2003 the Israeli prime minister Ariel Sharon met with his education minister Limor Livnat to ask her to reinforce the history and civic studies textbooks with references to "our ownership of the land of Israel over history" and with "proofs that Jews did not conquer or occupy the land but only came back after a long exile."[13]

This may be an inert process of reflecting social perceptions on good citizenship; however, some of its components can be traced back to conscious efforts to reinforce a militaristic form of patriotism made in the early days of the state of Israel. In 1950, Chief of Staff Yigael Yadin appeared before the Teachers' Council on behalf of the Jewish National Fund (the main educational body in the Israeli community before statehood and one of the main bodies in formulating education policy in the early days of the state). As part of his attempt to make the army the focal point of Zionist education in the state, Yadin declared: "The questions in mathematics should not deal with the merchant who sells wine or oil, but rather with a plane that takes off from Base A and a second that takes off from Base B, and at what speed the second has to fly to overtake the first."[14] The aim was to create a military

41

perspective even in academic subjects that do not deal directly with the history of the Jewish people. The children's thoughts, discourse, and imagination were to be molded in light of what the young state needs in order to survive.

In 1951 the Teachers' Council considered the goals of education. "The main proposal that was discussed at the conference was to place the Israel Defense Forces, the army of the people, at the center of Zionist education in the state. The first initiative on this matter came from the Hasbara [Information] Department in the Ministry of Defense."

The director of the Education Department specified main attributes of the desirable citizen, the first of which was "the Israeli individual's identification with society: we must suppress any manifestation of isolationism and detachment from the public and instead develop the civic-political sense that atrophied among us under the cloak of the Exile; we must educate for citizenship in accepting the authority of the state, for discipline in patriotism including the sacrifice of one's life on the altar of freedom, nationality, and political independence."[15]

With the establishment of the state of Israel, the education system was thus made responsible for molding citizens who would carry the burden of safeguarding the young state's security. The ideal graduate of the school is not measured (or only marginally so) by the extent of her commitment to democracy, or by her capacity for critical thinking, or by her attitude toward pluralism—to mention only a few of the traits that civic education ideally seeks to cultivate. Since its earliest days, the focus in the Israeli education system has been on how to produce citizen-warriors. Today the Israeli education system's approach holds dear the belief that it must contribute its part to creating citizens who are capable, and desirous, of playing as active a role as possible in defending the state. It reflects the public conception of the good citizen as one who holds the needed attitudes for confronting a protracted conflict, whose worldview will enable him to persevere in difficult periods of threat while maintaining the belief that victory is promised to the side that is just, namely, one's own side. The education system thus strives to inculcate citizenship as national identity, leaving little room for learning critical thought or democratic values and norms.

The expectation of peace is hardly a part of the worldview of the graduates of the Israeli education system. Peace, to the extent that the system addresses it, is presented as a utopia, a dream (and the fact that the Hebrew words for peace (*Shalom*) and dream (*Chalom*) rhyme does its share to further this attitude). The enemy is not associated in any clear way with the "dream of peace," and the imaginary era in which wars will cease refers only in some obscure way to the "bloodthirsty nations" and "inflamed masses" that have risen up to destroy the Jews in the past and the present, according to the common depiction in the history curriculum. The path to peace, the necessary compromises, the mutual and sympathetic learning about the (former) enemy (for purposes other than intelligence gathering)—none of these is systematically presented.

The utmost emphasis of the curriculum is on the two first components mentioned here as aspects of the civic education curriculum, namely, formal teaching of processes, and nationalism and patriotic sentiments. Very little is done to reinforce the third, and crucial, component of democratic sentiments and attitudes, or to introduce understanding of peace and how it can be achieved. Patriotic education is thus the central aspect of creating citizens in times of war, and the "patriotism" in this education is narrowly conceived as an uncritical endorsement of nationalism as part of one's identity. How is patriotic education conceived of in the political and educational debate? How and in what form can it be justified, if at all? The next section looks at these questions.

RECONCILING DEMOCRACY WITH PATRIOTIC EDUCATION? CHALLENGES OF WARTIME

The debate on the justifications and proper modes of patriotic education is not reserved for wartime alone. Scholars and educators in democratic countries debate the role of the state in inducing, through its public education system, the values and sentiments that mark committed members of the nation. Proponents of patriotic education tend to support the installment of a special sense of identification with one's country and compatriots, which in some cases inclines one to give them prior consideration. Instilling such sentiments can be a consequence of teaching "noble, moralizing history."[16] Authors from William Galston to Richard Rorty, from Arthur Schlesinger to Robert Fullinwider to Eamonn Callan have argued for teaching patriotism in public schools, mainly through the history curriculum.[17] The main idea is that future citizens must learn to love and honor their country if they are to become good members of society, if they are to defend it when necessary and give it precedence over their own or their group's narrower interests. Most of these arguments are based on conceiving of citizenship and national affiliation as an identity-related matter, and hence regarding patriotism as a legitimate form of identity formation and expression.

The main questions liberal authors grapple with in this context are, how compatible is patriotism with justice and democracy? And when they collide, which is to take precedence? A widely accepted notion is that "civic education limited to inculcation of traditional patriotism or conventionalist ideology" is "inadequate for an advanced industrial society."[18] For some critics, patriotism is merely "a primordial attachment to a territory and a society,"[19] which may not be an appropriate educational aim. Indeed, some suggest that a proper educational aim would be to overcome such primordial emotions, and to train future citizens to rely more on their reason and less on urges in making political choices. Following the Kantian tradition, some contemporary liberal (and radical) authors suggest that education should aim at overcoming national attachments, whether in favor of cosmopolitan affiliation or of an individualized, "unencumbered" self.[20]

National sentiments are not based on truisms or on descriptions of history that aim to correspond with established facts. National sentiments—as the notion itself hints—are focused less on justifications and more on the emotions they cultivate. Teaching patriotism can thus elevate the nation-state's values or perspectives over those of its subgroups and neighbors. Consequently, some claim that history teachers should direct their efforts not to the teaching of patriotism at all, but to the presentation of a variety of accurate and responsible perspectives on historical events. The aim should be the development of appropriate knowledge of the nation's history, or in Harry Brighouse's words, "teaching what happened and teaching them skills essential to figuring out why."[21]

As noble as this aim may sound from a liberal rational perspective, I suspect it may not satisfy the demands, and the needs, of nations at war. I sympathize with Brighouse's claim that for the most part, patriotism should not be an aim of the public education system, although it can be a recognized (or controlled) side effect of proper schooling. However, the special identification with one's country is not only a sentimental response to security threats (although it is partly that, too). It is also a sociopsychological mechanism for sustaining the strain conflict creates. Dismissing these sentiments or ignoring them in the classroom may create antagonism, it may backfire, or it may render the civic educational effort detached and irrelevant. It would be more useful as well as justified to work *with* the national sentiments (rather than against them or apart from them). This is even more important in wartime than in peaceful eras, for those emotions take a more central place in the public life of a nation at war, serving the needs of endurance through periods of uncertainty and threats.

Hence, the demand to dismiss patriotic and national sentiment in favor of cosmopolitanism, liberal individualism, or fact-based rational debate is not practicable at any time, and more forcefully so in times of war. This impracticability makes those trends undesirable as educational aims, for they work against psychological and moral realities. The teaching of national sentiments and patriotism should be accepted as part of the curriculum. How, then, can liberal authors reconcile patriotism and nationalism with the civic-democratic aims of education? Some authors suggest separating "national sentiment" or "patriotism" from "nationalism," arguing that the former are adequate aims for public schooling, for they foster the students' existing affiliations with their community without the idea that this community is better than others, an idea that is associated with the latter. Patriotism, Gutmann reminds us, "is a sentiment rather than a moral perspective."[22] To properly respond to this sentiment in the context of education, theorists should not (and usually do not) defend it in its basic expression of "my country, right or wrong." This would create a risk of uncritical acceptance of wrongful actions by the state. "A

45

democratic education opposes this kind of patriotism when it encourages students to think about their collective lives in morally principled terms."[23] Callan, Tamir, and Miller have all defended various forms of this compatibility thesis, arguing that democracy and national sentiment can in fact reinforce each other when properly constructed as educational aims. Miller regards this version of nationalism as coinciding with the basic requirements of both democratic values and principles of justice.[24] Tamir offers a liberal version of nationalism that enables citizens and educators to foster a national sentiment that does not clash with the liberal-democratic ideal.[25] National sentiment, according to these scholars, does not necessarily rely on complete falsehoods, and therefore it does not utterly contradict rational demands. This is an attempt to construct a version of national sentiment, or patriotism, which is compatible with liberal justice and hence may serve as an adequate educational aim. This argument advocates teaching patriotism by suggesting that we need to teach students that they (we) have special obligations toward our compatriots because we share the same political fate. Our decisions and choices, because of the nature of democracy, influence the lives and opportunities of those who share our nationality.[26] This argument goes part of the way toward establishing the claim for teaching citizenship and patriotism as derivative of shared fate. However, it relies on a restricted content of this shared fate, as related solely to democratic choices and isolated from historical narration or a sense of identity. Consequently, it loses sight of some of the deeper sentiments associated with communal affiliations and renders itself only partially relevant to the moral realities it aims to respond to and affect. This liberal argument validates the teaching of proper deliberative skills, but it does not add up to a satisfactory rationale for teaching patriotism, neither from the logical nor from the sociological perspective. Logically speaking, if decisions taken by any individual in a specific group affect the other members of the group, then individuals need to learn to coordinate their choices, to be tolerant to dissent, and to listen to other opinions in the group. They may need to learn to give voice to other members who are not initially heard. There may be a need to limit the scope of decisions so that certain elements that are crucial to individual well-being—let us call them basic rights—are not steamrolled over in the process of decision making. But all this can be satisfied through learning the processes and principles of deliberative democracy, and by ensuring the adequate functioning of democratic institutions. No national sentiment must come into the picture, and no preference has to be given to the members of the group—the compatriots—in terms of personal affiliation or solidarity.

From a social perspective too, the claim from mutual effect to teaching patriotism does not suffice. Actions taken by certain nation-states, or groups within them, can and do influence many others who are not invited to be part of the decision-making process. The easiest case to make here is the environmental one: decisions regarding deforestation, pollution of the seas or air, genetic modification of foods, or financing the research and development of new medications can be detrimental or beneficial to nonmembers as well as to members of the nation-state who make the call on these issues. Waging a war is another example of a decision that has a significant effect on the lives of those people who could not be part of the process of deliberation (if it took place) and decision making.

Moreover, it is unclear if the liberal versions of national sentiment correspond with the needs that motivate patriotism. The persistence of the crude and supremacist versions of patriotism and nationalism in the international arena suggests that maybe the tamed versions cannot suffice as a unifying notion of common purpose. Moreover, teaching patriotism as a way of advancing stability through fostering mutual trust among compatriots, as Callan suggests, can be contradictory to claims of justice and critical thinking even in peaceful times. In wartime this type of argumentation can more readily become detrimental to the dual causes of democracy and peace. Stability may indeed be important in many occasions in a nation's history, but in time of conflict this concept easily becomes synonymous to uncritical thinking, rigidity, and lack of alternative visions of the future. It too easily feeds into the belligerent conceptions of patriotism, and into the rigid notions of national unity as a given identity that sustains these conceptions over time.

To summarize the discussion so far, it is impracticable as well as undesirable to dismiss the teaching of patriotism altogether; however, many attempts to point at the compatibility of patriotism with other liberal educational aims put too much emphasis on aspects of citizenship and nationalism that fail to correspond with expressed social expectations of both peace and wartime. Many of the flaws associated with the liberal argument for patriotic education arise because of the underlying assumption of citizenship as identity. Conceptualizing national affiliation as an essential (or inherent) component of an individual's and a group's identity is the source of the arguments criticized above, that educators should foster the students' existing affiliations with their communities or work to establish trust and special preference toward one's compatriots. The claim that conceptualizing citizenship as shared fate rather than solely as identity offers a more adequate basis for justifying (and restructuring) the teaching of patriotism in schools. Expansive education thus goes a step further than the common liberal argument by endorsing the teaching of patriotism that would be informed by citizenship not only as an aspect of identity but also as deriving from the shared fate of all fellow nationals. The crux of the argument is that the diversification of the conceptions of patriotism, which is a result of understanding citizenship as shared fate, opens the way to endorsing the productive aspects of belligerent citizenship while maintaining a strong commitment to democratic values (and thus rejecting the undesirable aspects of belligerent citizenship). This argument, which is one of the main aspects of expansive education, may encounter some hurdles on its way to the classroom. The next section illustrates how perspectives on patriotic education are influenced by security threats and conflict, as portrayed by the American debate on teaching history after 9/11.

Teaching History in Times of War: The Post–9/11 American Debate

The challenges educators and scholars regularly face in the realm of patriotic education are posed with a greater sense of urgency in times of conflict, when patriotism is perceived as a national security matter. As stated in the opening remarks of *Education for Democracy*, a study by the Albert Shanker Institute, after September 11 "[t]he issue of defending our democracy was no longer an abstraction, the question of civic education no longer an option."[27] "It may be," the study continues, "that September 11 presents us with a moment, an opportunity for civic renewal."[28]

In a review of history textbooks published by the conservative Fordham Foundation, Chester E. Finn Jr. laments the use of third person language in describing historical events, such as portraying 9/11 as a "tragedy" that "happened":

> I've dubbed such verb usages the "irresponsible impersonal" voice and, regrettably, they're more norm than exception in U.S. history textbooks. . . . [T]hings happen in these books (though not necessarily in chronological order), but not because anybody causes them. Hence, nobody deserves admiration or contempt for having done something incredibly wonderful or abominably evil. . . . The result: . . . a collective loss of American memory.[29]

Finn is disheartened by this form of history he finds in high school textbooks because he worries that these books commonly fail to "establish a narrative of events with a strong sense of context." Other studies expressed similar concern before 9/11: "Faith in progress and patriotic pride have vanished" bemoans a 2000 report on history textbooks.[30]

Authors like Noam Chomsky and Henry Giroux, however, have been warning against the stifling effects of the same patriotic pride that Finn wishes for, in times of peace and even more urgently in times of conflict. Where Finn (and other conservative commentators) finds no sense of cause and an alarming loss of national pride, Chomsky (and other left-wing commentators) sees a vehement attack on democratic ideals through the uncritical endorsement of patriotism. In June 1999 Chomsky commented: "True democratic teaching is not about instilling patriotism."[31] In a similar vein, Giroux criticizes the blunt response of the American administration and public sphere to the September 11 attacks and the fear and hatred they brood. In an all-encompassing critique of the rise of patriotic pride, the attack on free speech, the threat on academic freedom, and other disconcerting effects, Giroux argues that "ignorance and arrogance are no substitute for reasoned analyses, critical understanding, and an affirmation of democratic principles of social justice."[32]

These two contrasting perspectives suggest that the teaching of patriotism either should be endorsed without question, through the narrowest understanding of the term, or should be rejected as a jingoistic attempt to quell legitimate political criticism and independent thought. Because these perspectives are some of the most visible in the field, many history teachers and school administrators find it hard to navigate between the two, sensing that these are the only alternatives. Teachers considering the liberal perspective such as that of Giroux or James Loewen[33] and the conservative one such as Finn's or Diane Ravitch's[34] have a hard time figuring out what students should ideally know about the nation's history. The first accuses existing history textbooks and standards as overpatriotic, shallowly optimistic, and hero-worshiping; the second warns against the tendency to reduce history to a narrow list of disconnected facts that are so focused on equal representation that they fail to convey any sense of national narrative. Both reject "ideology" as an unfit component for textbooks and classroom interaction, and insist that teaching materials should steer clear of ideological partialities. The navigation between the bluntly termed "liberal" and "conservative" conceptions of history and history teaching becomes more acute in times of national conflict, when teaching the "correct form" of history or inculcating the "required values"—whether liberal commitments to civil liberties or conservative forms of patriotism—is deemed essential to national survival. In another widely circulated publication of the Fordham Foundation, Sheldon Stern claims that "[i]n the wake of September 11," the influence of liberal scholars and authors is "more destructive than ever." He explains:

> Young Americans are being consciously taught to hate and be ashamed of their nation's history and to believe that America is a uniquely evil and oppressive society.[35]

Thus, most available texts, including the publications cited above, offer a strict choice between "moral relativism" and "moral clarity" if they are conservative, or between "critical thought" and "jingoism" if they are liberal. There is no need here for a detailed exploration of the reasons why critical thinking does not have to amount to moral relativism, in which any "opinion—yours, mine, Osama Bin-Laden's"[36] is similarly respected, and why a call for a contextual understanding of history through various tools, including heroic tales, does not have to amount to "lies my teachers told me." Clearly, what educators and educational administrators could use is a nuanced, contextualized discussion of patriotism in times of conflict and beyond. In the context of conflict, the need to endorse an expansive notion of education becomes more pressing as the list of topics considered worthy of public debate narrows, along with the scope of perspectives on those topics. The expansive form of civic education is aimed at strengthening attitudes necessary for national survival, in both the short- and long-term sense. The more immediate or short-term aims of survival and endurance require learning to feel and be united as a nation, believing in the just causes that guide the nation, and endorsing a positive version of its narrative—in short, they require patriotic unity. The long-term values and perceptions required for national endurance in times of conflict are primarily related to democratic principles, practices, and commitments. Both types of aims must be endorsed for civic education to be worthwhile, particularly in times of war. Abandoning the short-term aims may increase society's vulnerability and weaken the perseverance powers of the nation and its members. Abandoning the long-term aims may render the nation vulnerable to a diminished sense of purpose and result in a decline in civic engagement and a lack of common political ground.

The teaching of a sentimental history or a national narrative may seem to offer a satisfactory response to both liberal and national demands. It could focus students' attention on the national story of their community while encouraging them to endorse their existing affiliation to the group. Such endorsement, according to defenders of the compatibility thesis, should not take place at the expense of democratic affiliations. Rogan Kersh, for example, suggests that "any project promoting responsible citizenship must address issues of *national* belonging in explicit detail."[37] However, this perspective cannot offer an appropriate solution to the problem at hand, namely, the inclusion of both democratic perspectives and patriotic affiliations in the teaching of civics and history. First, the teaching of sentimental history goes against teaching critical thinking and even against the very notion of autonomy. As Brighouse convincingly claims, "[The state] wrongs the child by conditioning his or her consent to the

state, thus jeopardizing his or her ability to give the freely offered consent that is the marker of liberal legitimacy."[38] Many
have argued similarly about the teaching of patriotism as well
as autonomy—that by cultivating it, the state may undermine
its own legitimacy. That is because legitimacy has to rest on a
consent given autonomously by the citizens. When the conditions for this consent are instilled by the state, the consent can
hardly be regarded as free and thus does not suffice as a legiti-
mizing factor.

In addition, teaching sentimental history is both politically
and pragmatically flawed. It is politically unwarranted because
it tends to silence dissenting perspectives of history and thus
suppress pluralism for the sake of expressing a narrow and shal-
low notion of patriotic pride. It is pragmatically flawed because
teaching a noble version of history, creating a pantheon of heroes
that are expected to confer legitimacy on the state's institutions
(as Galston suggests), stands a grave risk of promoting, in the
long run, the opposite sentiments that it sets out to promote. The
"spirit of detached spectatorship" that Rorty laments,[39] the "cyn-
icism that sugar-coated history produces when youngsters get
older,"[40] results from the sobering realization of the complexities
of history that were concealed by both teachers and textbooks.
This change in perspective that happens to students often at a
later stage in their studies can render them cynical, detached, or
hostile to the aims of their patriotic education.

So much may be true in peace as much as in wartime. But
wartime creates further challenges to the possibility of convergence among civic education, patriotic education (or the inculcation of national sentiments), and democratic education. The fundamental challenge that wartime presents to the education
system is that of preserving democratic commitments. The propensity of citizens and government alike during wartime is to
waive or suspend some of their democratic commitments in lieu
of security concerns. The focal point of the relations between
government and civil society changes in the direction of greater
expectations from citizens to contribute to the state; a diminished public agenda and a restricted public deliberation; and
lack of transparency and a weakened commitment to civic liberties. Confronting these problematic aspects of democratic citizenship with a sentimental version of national history does not

seem to be a promising educational endeavor. The attempt to unite the citizenry in patriotic allegiance presupposes a conception of citizenship as an aspect of personal and group identity. It assumes a unified understanding of national identity, history, and tradition.[41] This presupposition goes not only against pluralism but also against the democratic and patriotic aims of expansive education. If we are to teach citizenship as shared fate—thus expanding the study of civic education to include both patriotism and democratic values—we cannot rely on the determinate traditions that provide the basis for the sentimental teaching of history.

Moreover, teaching sentimental versions of history goes against the common good and national interests, by way of enhancing the endorsement of the war culture. The education system has long been charged as a leading cause of the perseverance of war.[42] In 1926, Jonathan Scott wrote: "It may be that nationalistic education is the chief underlying cause of the war."[43] A decade later, Arthur Schlesinger observed: "Among the possible causes of war, education holds a particular and significant place . . . for in so far as it embodies dangerous nationalistic prejudices, it is a means of disseminating them constantly to all the people. It is the seed of international discord for both present and future generations."[44] Ruth Firer eloquently demonstrates how education, as a "part of any hegemonic culture, very often reflect[s] and reproduce[s] it."[45] Firer demonstrates how Israeli textbooks and curricular guidelines have such a perpetuating effect in circumstances of war. By failing to balance the social need of unity and mutual support, expressed by the narrowing conception of patriotism, with the requirement of preserving a democratic public sphere, the education system contributes to the war culture and thus betrays the long-term interests of society in maintaining its value structure.

Alternatively, by teaching citizenship and nationalism as shared fate, the public education system can endorse the long-term democratic aims of public education while supporting the short-term needs of belligerent citizenship. This approach would mandate teaching history through a nuanced understanding of nationhood as a mutual social construct that is both informed by and constructive of individual and group identity.[46] This constructive suggestion is meant to foster unity without abandoning critical perspectives and to teach wider, more flexible forms of patriotism that still satisfy the moral realities and social expectations of wartime. Teaching a pluralist version of history that endorses national identification has to be practiced with a background understanding of nationhood as a communal, historical enterprise of shared fate. It requires constructing the curriculum with an understanding of citizenship and national affiliation not only as a given, essential part of an individual's identity, but also as part of her fate as shared with other members of her community. As this is a more flexible conception of national affiliation, it allows for accommodations of various subgroups and diverse narratives into the teaching of history (and civics). While pluralistic and diverse, it does not shy away from fostering patriotism as an integral part of public education, with the understanding that some periods in a nation's existence—such as wartime—give rise to further emphasis on this aspect of education. Even in such times, however, critical thought—and even more so, pluralism—need not be abandoned, for the shared fate of the national group corresponds with the diverse aims of the groups that make up the nation. In other words, when patriotism is derivative not of identity but of shared fate, it can be taught as a flexible notion that accommodates (somewhat softer versions of) both liberal-democratic and conservative perspectives.

Conclusion

What are the needs of a society at war as they pertain to the education system? Perseverance can be determined as any society's basic interest. However, in war the implications of this interest in the political sphere are blurred; additionally, the educational implications of this prerequisite can vary widely. What does it mean for a society to survive? The survival of a group is, in a sense, a metaphor as long as physical extinction of all members is not an immediate threat; the focus of the discussion of group survival is commonly cultural rather than physical. What is at stake is the survival of the national or cultural group as it exists at present. This is the source of the prerequisite to preserve the social structure, the core values, or the political ideology that represents the group's "spirit." The need to preserve society as it is, including the social ability to reconstruct and critically reform itself through its proper institutions, is part of the quest for survival, second only to actual physical survival of the nation.

The crude educational interpretation of the quest for national survival is manifested in the wartime argument that the state, in order to survive, needs to cultivate in future citizens the emotional disposition that would enable them—even compel them—to defend their country. Some may claim (like the authors of the report quoted in the beginning of this chapter) that even if patriotic education is untenable in times of peace, the unique circumstances of conflict call for its endorsement because it may help support the country through the challenges of war. This argument represents one of the undesirable aspects of belligerent citizenship. The espousal of unifying patriotism and other aspects of belligerent citizenship by the public education system is perilous because it impedes democratic justice and replicates the circumstances of conflict. The public education system should never be made responsible for creating soldiers. Creating citizens is the first and foremost responsibility of a public education system in a democratic country. This role entails facilitating democratic inclinations, not enlisting students for their future roles as fighters. A country that aims to maintain the democratic commitments of its citizenry in order to ensure the perseverance of democracy through times of conflict (or recession, civic frictions, and other hardships) can never subordinate these "long range values," even in the face of the "life-and-death needs of today and tomorrow."[47] The pressures that the public puts before the education system to produce citizen-warriors, to inculcate the values of narrow patriotic unity, to suppress dissenting voices, should be balanced with an unwavering commitment to democracy on the part of the education system. Preserving democracy can go hand in hand with endorsing a public historical understanding of national membership as shared fate. It should be understood and practiced in the context of war as a commitment of the public education system to work with the more productive aspects of belligerent citizenship to support endurance while maintaining democratic affiliations. Thus, the teaching of patriotism as discussed in this chapter should not be abandoned but rather expanded to include further perspectives (one such

Peace Education: Anger Management and Care for the Earth

> Peace the great meaning has not been defined.
> When we say peace as a word, war
> As a flare of fire leaps across our eyes.
> We went to this school. Think war;
> Cancel war, we were taught.
> What is left is peace.
> No, peace is not left, it is no canceling.
> —Muriel Rukeyser, *Peace the Great Meaning*

WAR AND PEACE are blurred in today's world, and it is often hard to tell when a war is declared, what would be the effect of a peace treaty and, most crucially, how a nation is to prepare for either of them. The possibility of a cold war and a protracted war on terrorism make it hard to properly define and contextualize both military actions and attempts to achieve peace. It is hard to separate "peacekeeping forces" from military troops, hard to decide what qualifies as a preemptive measure or national self-defense. This is not merely a problem of Newspeak. It is a matter of emerging political relations among nations, groups, and organizations that are less clearly defined than "war" and "peace." Nonetheless, in this blurry context, striving toward structuring social tools designed to foster peaceful relations is vital. The subsequent attempt to design and implement peace studies curricula in schools is part and parcel of the project of peace building. Diplomacy alone, while important, is not sufficient. The citizens must learn to aspire to, embrace, and endure the road for peace.

Peace scholars and educators have been pondering these issues for decades. After World War II, many educators—most of them Europeans—pioneered an effort to establish a humanistic theory and practice of peace education. The scholarly and pedagogic efforts to respond to the ever-changing political realm of war and peace continued in the fields of international relations and education.

Beyond navigating the challenges of the changing world order, peace scholars need to grapple with the psychological and cognitive complexities of conceptualizations of war and peace. Educating for peace is complicated by the suggestion that understanding the concept "peace" is developed only as a second-order formulation in children's minds, derivative to the concept "war." As a more concrete concept, war is easier to grasp, whereas peace, if it is not perceived solely as a negation of war (as indeed it should not be), is a more abstract notion that requires maturity and further cognitive effort to develop.[1]

Expansive education aims to respond to these psycho-political challenges through pedagogic and curricular means. Peace studies, and in particular peace education, may seem an obvious field to turn to in search of perspectives that could inform and enrich expansive education. However, despite its promising title and framework, the field of peace education suffers from numerous flaws that impair its ability to adequately address the complexities of civic education in wartime. Expansive education includes a dual focus—peace and democracy—but even its peace-related aspect is not appropriately addressed in the peace education field. The key deficiency of the theoretical and pedagogic accounts of peace education is their reluctance to treat peace and war as political categories that should be responded to mainly with civic tools. Consequently, the main contribution of this field to the structuring of an informed expansive education is not in theoretical and analytic perspective, but rather in some of the practical pedagogic tools developed through years of field work.

Peace education "is not just anti-war education."[2] Johan Galtung, one of the founders of the field, has offered a distinction between negative peace—the absence of war and violence—and positive peace, which refers to the existence of economic, cultural, and political practices that contribute to the well-being of the citizens on all sides.[3] In Israel this distinction is commonly described by the terms "cold peace" and "warm peace," the former relating to relations (such as between Israel and Egypt since

1979) in which no open hostilities occur, but hardly any economic and cultural relations are formed either. Warm peace entails normalized relations between former enemies, including economic, intellectual, and other contacts. Constructive approaches of peace education commonly focus on supporting through education the social conditions that generate positive peace.

The originating question in the field of peace education is a broad one: how should the education system respond to circumstances of war in a manner that could promote the possibility of peace? Surveying the scholarly work on peace education and its research, one encounters a disconcerting phenomenon. The variety of seemingly unrelated subjects amalgamated under the heading "peace education"—women's rights and economic equality, anger management and environmental awareness, acceptance of "others" and their narratives, and subscribing to the meta-narrative of universal human rights—all of these are promoted with a similar sense of urgency and goodwill. Few of the approaches devote any attention to civic and political factors.

A number of criteria can be used to analyze the content of peace education as a field of practice. One of the most influential categorization is the geographic one. Gavriel Salomon, a leading Israeli scholar, categorizes existing peace education programs according to the region in which they are practiced. The challenges that peace educators face, their goals, and their responses to the participants or students vary dramatically according to the political circumstances in which they function. Comparative psychological studies on children, performed in the same regions during peaceful times and times of conflict, as well as the comparison between peaceful regions and regions in conflict (such as between Dutch and Palestinian children), suggest significant differences.[4] Comparing peace education efforts around the world, Salomon claims that whereas "regions of relative tranquility emphasize education for cooperation and harmony, promoting the idea of a general culture of peace, regions of conflict emphasize education for violence prevention" and other negative accounts of peace.[5] These different emphases are warranted by the different experiences and derivative conceptual backgrounds of the students. Salomon convincingly argues that although various distinctions have great theoretical importance,

59

"the socio-political context in which peace education takes place supersedes the rest."[6] Martha Minow, too, differentiates between programs employed in "societies struggling to implement peace" and those practiced in "settings more remote from immediate conflict."[7]

The geographical criterion serves as the background for the current discussion, which examines approaches to peace education according to a related criterion, namely, the goals they set to achieve. The goals of peace education differ significantly between regions in conflict and peaceful regions. The criterion of declared aims helps to identify two common trends of thought and practice in the field, titled here the "pedagogic approach" and the "holistic approach." The pedagogic approach signifies a pragmatic attempt to offer a specific response to local, narrowly defined needs arising from conflict among groups or nations. The holistic approach is a broader attempt to reconstruct society as a nonviolent space. Focusing on their respective declared aims and subsequent analyses and constructive suggestions illustrates the foremost deficiency of peace education as a scholarly and practical field as undertaken by both approaches, namely, its apoliticization. This shortcoming will be shown to make most existing approaches to peace education less than relevant in answering the needs of a democratic society in conflict.

CAN'T WE ALL GET ALONG? THE PEDAGOGIC TREND IN PEACE EDUCATION

Minow offers a set of five approaches to what she calls "education for co-existence." The approaches she describes are "education in conflict resolution; education through social contact; education in human rights; education in moral reasoning; and education in the histories of intergroup conflicts."[8] The first two approaches constitute hands-on strategies to teach students how to cooperate with others, whether they are classmates (the emphasis in most conflict resolution programs) or members of an adversary group. Two other approaches Minow mentions mainly comprise an academic exposition of topics related to conflict—namely, human rights and the conflict in which the students' group is involved. The approach that focuses on moral reasoning, the most abstract one, aims at teaching acknowledg-ment and understanding of the "other" through a universalized strategy of argumentation for opposing positions. Although these approaches differ significantly, they all fit under the cur-rent heading of the "pedagogic approach," for they generally ac-cept the mainstream description (or narrative) of social or inter-national conflict and attempt to offer direct pedagogic responses to what they view as the social requirements for achieving peace. Thus, if conflict is understood as perpetuated by lack of intergroup contact, organized encounters are offered; if extrem-ism is viewed as arising from flaws in critical thinking, students are invited to participate in courses in moral reasoning.[9]

Broadly speaking, the pedagogic approach in peace education represents a pragmatic, localized response to the challenges of striving for peace by educational means. It mostly comprises specified knowledge and strategies and tends to focus on the de-velopment of identifiable capacities, such as conflict resolution and anger management skills. The pedagogic approach can be found both in regions immersed in conflict and in those living in relative tranquility, although there too it is commonly offered as a cure to local needs, such as racial tension. In different places the pedagogic approach generates distinct curricular materials, according to the conflict-related challenges it faces: in the South African context, peace education entails mostly educating against racism, and toward reconciliation among oppressor and op-pressed, who should learn to live together in a new era of (at least formal) equality.[10] As such, it carries many traits of multicultural education, without the temporal aspects of peace education in a region in conflict. In the American context the focus is often on personal relations and conflict resolution skills.[11] In the Israeli context, the pedagogy of peace education is manifested in creat-ing structured opportunities for group contact, and in attempts to cultivate basic recognition of the humanity of the "other."

Authors working in relatively disillusioning political environ-ments, such as Ruth Firer (from Israel), Maria Hadjipavlou-Tri-georgis, (from Cyprus), Dinka Čorkalo (from Croatia), and Ce-cile Mukarubuga (from South Africa), among others,[12] share a narrower conception of the peace to which they aspire. Al-though they differ significantly in their methodologies and perspectives, they tend to have one thing in common: modesty of aspiration. They seem to hope for no more than an ending to explicit intergroup violence, and even that seems to be out of reach in many regions. In this trend, cessation of violence supercedes all other aims, and thus the authors focus on pragmatic, pedagogic tools to promote this concrete aim. In other cases, pedagogic approaches, mostly when practiced in more tranquil regions, focus on an attempt to improve and pacify interpersonal relations, with little attention to the international relations field.[13] "Conflict resolution programs usually focus . . . on developing students' abilities to avoid conflicts and mediate them."[14] These curricula, while directly working toward the reduction of interpersonal violence, work in light of a conception of "peace" that is merely personal or, at best, civic. "Conflict" in this description refers to peer relations rather than to international relations. It may, in its best forms, strive to create conditions that could enable or facilitate deliberation in the public sphere. But usually it has little to do with fostering or promoting peace in its political sense.

In war-ridden regions, where students experience conflict not only in their relations with their peers but also in their daily encounters with security measures, expressions of organized violence, and media representations of local war, some pedagogic programs respond by offering intergroup encounters. This approach is more feasible for Israelis and Palestinians or for the opposing sides in Northern Ireland or in Cyprus than for, say, Americans and Iraqis, because of the geographic proximity of the enemy. Such programs are based on the rationale that "through intergroup contact, people who belong to different . . . groups can overcome stereotypes, develop positive cooperative experiences, and exemplify relationships of equality and mutual acceptance."[15] Through programs of intergroup encounters, educators hope to achieve further understanding and establish personal relations that can potentially overcome animosity. However, personal encounters between members of adversary groups do little to change the attitudes of the participants, let alone influence the reality of the conflict itself.[16] Studies show that personal contacts can generate change in prejudicial attitudes in marginal ways,[17] as well as promote the skills necessary for good, friendly personal relations with one's peers. But their influence usually fades when these same young people, once they graduate from high school, return to their homogeneous environments, as is common in conflicting regions, or—as in Israel/Palestine—are sent to look at their peers through the sights of a gun.

The most apparent deficiency of this trend in both tranquil and conflicting regions is its lack of political contextuality: the pedagogic approach usually fails to analyze the moral-political circumstances and consequences of war and peace. Peace educators and curriculum designers who work within the pedagogic trend portray a narrow conception of conflict, and as a result focus on offering techniques for the "reduction of violence."[18] The attempt to teach students means of avoiding conflict or resolving it relates to the context of peer relations in the classroom or schoolyard. These skills have little to do with the ability to avoid or solve conflicts in the international arena. In a sense, lumping "conflict resolution" programs under the heading of "peace education" is little more than a linguistic lapse. But this is not the whole story; the linkage between peer group conflicts and national conflicts is not merely a linguistic one. As we will see in the following section, this linkage is made by authors subscribing to other approaches as well, and they try to justify it with complex (though, I suggest, still mistaken) theoretical claims. The near-exclusive focus on personal relations—between peers sharing a classroom or youth from adversary groups being taught "how to get along"—represents a somewhat naïve conception of peace and of civil society's role in enabling it. These apolitical conceptions stem from a tendency to strictly contrast peace with war and violence (following the Dewey tradition), and to oversimplify the civic components of these sociopolitical notions. Structurally, the argument informing the pedagogic approach is one of universal rationalism, in which all individuals can "get along" if they let their innate powers of moral reasoning prevail over infantile urges and "bloody primitivism."[19] Scholars who subscribe to this framework fail to acknowledge the moral realties of nationalism, and thus tend to focus their attention on practical solutions. Consequently, this trend in peace education may be able to offer ad hoc tools for responding to specific local conflicts, but it falls short of addressing the more general problems of society's future in regard to national and international conflict.

The advantages of this trend should nevertheless be noted, both in the context of peaceful nations and in that of regions in conflict (these two contexts cannot always be easily distinguished). As some of the above-mentioned studies find, when undertaken in the context of local interracial and other subgroup disputes, peer-group tensions, and other smaller-scale conflicts, pedagogic approaches to peace education tend to reduce instances of violence and sometimes create a commitment to less violent group relations. Conflict resolution programs and intergroup meetings sometimes support more inclusive attitudes, at least in the immediate future (most studies have found that many of these programs do not have a long-term impact).

When undertaken in the context of national conflict, pedagogic responses to the challenges of peace education sometimes generate, or maintain, basic levels of willingness to accommodate peaceful solutions. They create more trust among peers from rival backgrounds and promote basic acknowledgment of the humanity of the "other," thus creating the basis for accepting peace, if it is achieved. In this way pedagogic, skill-oriented peace education prepares the ground for peace, in contradiction to most other curricular components that more readily adhere to the culture of war. This form of education, however, does not provide the proper skills for future citizens to actively support peace or act civically or politically to achieve it. To address the more complex political goal of peace, these pragmatic tools need to be adapted to a wider framework that includes education for political engagement and civic participation, along with other components of democratic education. Expansive education can thus be informed by the pedagogic approach's practical tools of educationally responding to conflict; those tools, however, must be supplemented by a much wider, long-term response that incorporates civic and political aspects of reconciliation and democracy.

Permeating Violence: The Holistic Approach to Peace Education

The other trend in the field of peace education, entitled here the "holistic approach," is composed of a host of responses to the main question of peace education, namely, how should the education system respond to circumstances of war in a manner that could promote the possibility of peace? Although this trend includes scholars and educators coming from a variety of theoretical backgrounds, they share an approach to analyzing the problems at hand and the subsequent form of solution they aim for. In their analysis, the characterization of violence is fairly broad, described as a fundamental phenomenon of human interaction on all levels. Consequently, scholars who endorse the holistic approach share the extensive aims they construe for the project of peace education.[20] In other words, this trend is characterized by the reconstruction of almost all social relations as power struggles, and by the propensity to label most of them as forms of conflict that must be overcome by educational means (if they can be overcome at all).

In describing the conditions of war and the social dimensions of violence, Birgit Brock-Utne portrays a continuum of violence, from the bedroom to the boardroom to the battlefield. In a construction typical for peace education scholars of this trend, she considers all violent manifestations and effects to be interconnected and suggests that the response to all forms of violence needs to be unified as well. As for the extensive aims, Brock-Utne uses Mario Borelli's approach to offer a comprehensive definition of peace:

> By *peace* we mean the absence of violence in any given society, both internal and external, direct and indirect. We further mean the nonviolent results of equality of rights, by which every member of that society, through nonviolent means, participated equally in the decisional power which regulates it, and the distribution of the resources which sustain it.[21]

This definition is largely typical of the holistic approach. Describing all forms of violence as conceptually or pragmatically linked provides the framework for constructing the aim of this trend of peace education, namely, to devise a comprehensive program to eliminate all aspects of violence.

Holistic peace scholars criticize what they regard as a lack of theoretical analysis in the field (a point well made), as well as the modernistic inclination to contrast war to peace without further qualifications. They justifiably criticize the oversimplification of the problem at hand by many authors from the pedagogic approach. But they err by making one of two conclusions. In their more modest form, they aim for no less than the elimination of all forms of violence, including inequality of rights and class (as a structural form of violence). In their more radical form, they conclude that peace is never an attainable option or, more radically, that peace is not a better option than war. Relying on Foucauldian and Frankfurt school theories, scholars in this trend deconstruct universal conceptions of the good, of human rights, and of peace itself, thereby denying any attempt to improve society or to contribute to a realistic (rather than utopian) better future. The very notions of improvement and progress are rejected as harmful modernist illusions, and with them the ability of citizens to influence political action. This rejection amalgamates most aspects of human existence, from the psychological, interpersonal, social, and civic to the global and environmental. The broad-ranging criticism against so many social practices and perspectives threatens to become uncritical by its sweeping, sometimes unqualified inclination to condemn any and all social and educational practices as damaging. As a result, this trend's educational force is limited to a meta-theoretical discussion of power and has little effect on students' conception of the political world and their own roles in it.

This critique of the holistic approach's theoretical basis does not imply that no connection exists among various forms of violence. Certainly, an individual psychological analysis may reveal links between experiencing violence (as perpetrator or victim) and replicating it in a host of contexts. In addition, a similarity in form and motivation exists between various types of violence and hate.[22] Thus patriarchalism, which feeds social tendencies to ignore (and thus permit) domestic violence, is related to militarism in many ways. However, this psychological and social evidence is far from suggestive that violence is a unified phenomenon; moreover, it offers no corroboration to the claim that all forms of violence can be overcome through a single mechanism, educational or other. Thus, declaring that the aim of peace education is to deal with all forms of violence is too vague to serve as a reliable educational guideline. The demand that education resist all forms of violence is a viable one. But a more thorough investigation into the connections among the various manifestations of violence is required. A comprehensive rejection of violence, albeit noble, contributes little to the educational effort to support peace.

A certain linguistic and expressive continuum can be traced, admittedly, from playground shoving, to domestic violence, to war. Individuals perform the violent acts in all those, and other, instances of aggression. One need not go back to Freud's depiction of our basic instincts to recognize that violence is indeed a prevalent social phenomenon. It should still be maintained, however, that the social context of various manifestations of violence can differ significantly, and so does the range of desirable responses, even if they all stem from the same type of frustration. Men who abuse their spouses are indeed acting in a violent, blameworthy manner. They fail to "manage" their anger or find legitimate modes for expressing their negative emotions. Some feminist activists even define the prevalent phenomenon of domestic violence as "terrorism," but again, despite the similarities (mainly related to living in fear), the analogy is a metaphor rather than a productive comparison. The mode of violence and its social context matter not only for the purpose of theoretical analysis, but even more crucially for devising relevant social and educational responses to address the violence.

Searching for a psychological response to permeating violence, Ervin Staub asks, "What are the cultural, social and psychological requirements for a peaceful world that nourishes the human spirit . . . ?"[23] The significance of recognizing common basic human needs—all that unites us as a species—is a major part of the driving force of many scholars who aim to overcome all forms of violence. Examining the psychological and sociopsychological conditions that facilitate war or peace is important for the formation of positive or "warm" peace. As Staub powerfully expresses, the frustration of basic human needs makes violence more likely and therefore makes peace harder to achieve. From this perspective, violence in all its forms results from the same social conditions. Peer violence in educational settings, domestic violence, hate crimes, social discrimination against women or minorities, war—all are the result of frustrated needs, and all can be overcome by the satisfaction of those needs through a unified social response.[24]

Henry Giroux offers a comparably broad account of the subject in his analysis of the effects of September 11 on American culture, in particular in the educational context. His convincing, detailed analysis of the burden that the attacks and the ensuing

war(s) put on American democracy is overshadowed by his unqualified response to the challenge. This response consists of an
attack on capitalism, on the rejection of popular culture in
schools, racial discrimination, gender inequality, and the failure
to understand patriotism as a culture of dissent that ideally fosters "access to health care, housing, food, meaningful employment, child-care education programs for all citizens."[25] Although
his perspective on how the militaristic culture stifles democratic
inclinations is well based, he fails to recognize the constructive
aspects of belligerent citizenship as differentiated from those aspects that imperil democracy. Consequently, his response is un-
focused, and as often happens with holistic approaches, it lumps
together a range of issues that are not necessarily related and
whose application in schools hardly tackles the requirements of
civic education in wartime and for peace.

In another notable example of the same trend, Betty Reardon
describes her aim as "mainstreaming peace and gender perspectives in education."[26] Her work addresses the methods by which
the formal education system can further the aims of peace and
gender equality. Education for a culture of peace is designed to
provide an "overarching concept under which the many and
varied topics and approaches that comprise the field can be integrated,"[27] and a culture of peace is described as "the humane
analogue of a healthy ecosystem composed of complementary,
functionally integrated forms of biodiversity."[28] Her book combines a concrete, detailed analysis of the social and political dimensions of educating for a culture of peace, with a utopian conceptualization of the peace in question. She recognizes the need
for "learning to take democratic responsibility for a peaceful
public order,"[29] and she even spells out the need to teach students nonviolent strategies that responsible democratic citizens
can use to oppose an unjust government. However, she devotes
very little discussion to the civic educational implications of this
claim. Reardon's book offers a comprehensive consideration of
the global, social, political, and personal dimensions of a culture
of peace, while also paying considerable attention to the gender
perspective of these various dimensions. In fact, the comprehen-
siveness of the approach is what undermines its pragmatic in-
tentions. Reardon suggests an approach that ties together so
many varied personal capacities—moral inclusion, celebration

of diversity, conflict resolution skills, care and hope, environmental awareness, and gender sensitivity, among still others— that the sum of them is lesser than its parts; it adds up to an impracticable conception of what a culture of peace means.

But Reardon herself warns that her book is offered as a prototype rather than a definitive text. Perhaps it would be possible for educators to excerpt the fundamentals of her perspective and amend them to their needs. Reardon states that personal relations within the classroom are "the most significant of all the factors involved in education for the formation of humane persons."[30] The educational effort to form "humane persons" was successfully realized, we are told, in the Norwegian UNESCO Associated School, where boys "have been weaned from competitive, aggressive behavior by learning that 'it's Fun to be Nice.'" Reardon notes that "were nations to learn this same lesson, there would be a culture of peace."[31] Aside from the principled deficiencies in a lesson plan that aims to teach that "it's Fun to be Nice," the more pressing problem is that the method of transition from the personal to the political and international realm is not clarified. We may assume that if all children were to be educated according to this (or a similar) study unit, they might contribute to the enhancement of a culture of peace in their communities and nations. But for that to happen, the public school system would have to endorse the program, which would mean that the political administration has already taken a significant step in the direction of subscribing to a culture of peace. Neglecting to consider nationalism and patriotism significantly reduces the relevance of this approach. Moreover, the fact that the successful experiment took place in a peaceful, democratic country like Norway also points to the necessity of having a differentiated and politically contextual account of peace education. That is especially true when the change in question is as comprehensive as the one Reardon advocates.

The political contextualization becomes even more vital when we recall that the holistic education approach is characteristic not only of academic scholarship but also of some leading world institutions. The constructive model that UNESCO describes as the basis of peace is no less comprehensive than the holistic critique: "Peace is incompatible with malnutrition, extreme poverty and the refusal of the rights of people to self-determination."[32] In 1978 the United Nations (UN) declared that peace

69

implies that every human being regardless of sex has the right to live in peace. Although these definitions are admittedly desirable, they are unclear as foundations for policies in general and for educational responses in particular. How are educators and curriculum designers to interpret the demand for elimination of poverty and human rights violations as a condition for peace?

From a philosophical perspective, the holistic approach is more plausible than the pedagogic "conflict resolution" or "anger management" approaches to peace education. For theoretical purposes as well as for the purpose of implementation in educational settings, it is crucial to analyze the terms used, the assumptions made, and the goals that go unstated or are taken for granted. The pedagogic attempt to offer an applicable framework generates a neglect of conceptual and even social foundations, which often renders it contradictory or oversimplified.

However, peace education is not a purely analytical project. At its best, peace education is a theoretical, pedagogic, and social enterprise, that aims to spark a cognitive as well as practical change for the better in society. These goals are hindered by the holistic approach because of its imbalance between theoretical analysis and pragmatic aims. This imbalance generates a definition of war and peace (or violence and nonviolence) in terms that, albeit philosophically defensible, are largely inapplicable to the social realm. For example, despite the conceptual link, intergroup violence can reside while domestic violence persists. For the sake of maintaining peace education as a theoretically sound as well as practically feasible approach, these manifestations of violence should not be regarded as one and the same.

This critique addresses the psychological, philosophical, and educational holistic approaches. When educators work toward creating the social conditions to achieve peace, recognizing human similarity across group difference cannot be a satisfactory aim. Clearly, it is important to recognize all individuals' psychological needs, as well as to make sure that their other human needs are not frustrated. Clearly, recognizing the equal humanity of the "other" or the enemy is crucial. Ideally, educating a generation of future citizens to fulfill their own as well as the others' need for healing, inclusive caring, supportive communities, and other aspects of nurturing cultures, as Staub suggests, can potentially promote national and international peaceful existence. It would be best if these educational processes took place on both or all adversary sides. But the road to achieve this aim is political rather than psychological. Intervention with psychological or interpersonal (sociopsychological) tools does not always have a significant impact even on school climate, not to mention long-term commitment to conflict resolution in the wider social realm.[33] For conflicting parties to be ready for peace, it is not enough that students foster an attitude of inclusive caring or of care and hope.[34] Students must learn to foster civic values and practices and maintain an empowered approach vis-à-vis the political establishment, the public agenda, and the taken-for-granted assumptions of the war culture, if they are to envision an alternative future and strive for it.

THE APOLITICIZATION OF PEACE EDUCATION

In 1999 the Hague Appeal for Peace Civil Society Conference proclaimed that systematic education for a culture of peace was necessary in order to bring about global circumstances that would facilitate the emergence of peace. Despite repeated affirmations of this claim in the past thirty years by various international organizations, the appeal states that "few educational institutions have undertaken such action."[35] Why is it that the noble causes of peace, democracy, equality, and human rights, so vigorously advocated by international institutions, so thoroughly examined in scholarly books, halt at the entrance to (or exit from) the classroom? Why is it that despite the variety of programs addressing numerous aspects of violence and antiviolence, culture of peace, healing processes, and reconciliation, "the slaughter continues"?[36] The reluctance of many peace educators and scholars to deal with the direct political requirements of peace education may offer some insight into the possible answer to this question. Over half a century ago, Maria Montessori claimed that when educators fail to politicize education in order to tailor a proper response to the circumstances of war, they in effect act in the service of the war culture. This claim seems to carry significant weight even today.

The most important issue to recognize when discussing possible responses to manifestations of violence is the sociopolitical structure in which the violence occurs. Peace building and peace education are informed by ideal notions of positive peace on the one hand and practical considerations of persisting conflict and violence on the other. "Peacebuilding," according to one account "is the practical interactive approach to the solving of the structural causes of violence and regenerating peaceful relations between people and communities which will convert confrontation and 'enemy images' into cooperation and partnership."[37] This concept was fostered by the United Nations as a comprehensive approach to international conflict resolution.[38] The project of peace building is thus both an analytic and a political one, and as such it strives to depict societal interests and aims, and to rely on theoretical analyses in order to devise tools for realizing those interests and aims.

In contrast to classroom or domestic violence, soldiers who are sent to war by their countries are hardly to blame for their violent acts. If they behave according to national and international codes of behavior and the *jus in bello* criteria—i.e., refrain from looting, raping, torturing, killing prisoners of war, and other unacceptable acts of violence—they are commonly praised for their heroic acts of violence toward enemy soldiers. Just War theory is aimed at suggesting the legitimate array of violent behaviors in war. It is the social context of war that creates the circumstances under which society permits certain violent acts to occur.

These circumstances are not always clear, and the criteria of moral behavior in the battlefield are continually debated. In war, says Michael Walzer, justice is under a cloud.[39] The very concepts of war, peace, and peace processes are not neatly defined terms but murky, overlapping sociopolitical circumstances that are sometimes hard to tell apart. In Israel, as in the United States, one of the common debates in early 2002 centered on the queston "Are we in a state of war?" Legal and political analysts, as well as security experts, grappled with the question and could not reach a consensual answer. Some instances of war are more apparent than others, some conditions of violence are more evident than others, and it is indeed part of the philosopher's—and the educator's—responsibility to tackle these complexities.

By neglecting to address the political aspects of war and the quest for peace, educators will likely fail to accomplish the goals they set forth in peace education initiatives. This failure may result in education itself evolving into an act of "war by other means" (as suggested in chapter 2): education may as a matter of default replicate widespread beliefs about the inevitability of war or promote narrow notions of patriotism that obscure alternative visions of the future. This tendency is apparent in some forms of activism and thought in the field, such as the demand to maintain "peace through strength," which echoes the Roman tradition expressed in the phrase "Who desires peace, should prepare for war."

The holistic literature, with its postmodernist roots, tends to regard various expressions of violence as one and the same, and therefore attempts to overcome them through a change of personal and social perspectives. The direct political consequences of opposing war and fostering peace are obscured in these trends of thought by the simultaneous consideration of many forms of violence and the desirable responses to them. Political scientists who are conscious of the importance of nationalism in sociopolitical relations agree that civic education cannot be apolitical and remain effective: "The idea that the goals of civic education are to be equated with the totality of human interpersonal relations . . . such an approach is . . . too vague and general to be useful."[40]

The failure to envision a different future is the weakest side of existing peace education approaches of both trends. The reduction of peace to a utopian era of fluttering butterflies and economic profits, or alternatively to the direct continuation of placid personal relations, fails to become a suggestive alternative to a reality of violence and hatred. The movement from one level to the other is unclear in most peace education programs: how do citizens contribute to the continuation of violence or to its alteration? How can the enchanting image of peace be realized? How does one's serene solution to personal differences with one's peers turn out to be a factor in national conflicts? Absent responses to these questions peace education fails to tackle the rigidity and stagnation that are the hallmarks of belligerent citizenship.

The limitation of the two key approaches to peace education lies in their misrepresentation of the political nature of war, peace, and peace education. With the one trend focusing on the

micro level and the other aiming to deconstruct the political—
or to lump together all forms of violence without any ordering
or prioritizing—both approaches are unsatisfactory in creating
conscious political attitudes among future citizens.

In sum, most scholars and researchers in the peace education
field fail to address the direct political aspects of peace education.[41] Teaching peace education, or civic education in an orienta-
tion of peace, is a challenging process. Children learn to understand peace as an essential (rather than derivative) concept far
later than they grasp the meaning of war; in areas plagued by
conflict or where children experience the uncertainty and fear
related to fragile security circumstances, further cognitive, emotional and social obstacles converge on the path to educating for
a culture of peace.

Consequently, the contemporary scholarly and pedagogic field
of peace education is all too often based on definitions that are
either too broad or too narrow. Those who are affiliated with the
holistic trend describe "violence" as any instance of coercion, inequality, injustice, or structural hierarchy. Consequently, they
burden the field of peace education with too many hopes and
dreams, which, albeit admirable, cannot be satisfied all at once.
If "peace" means the disappearance of all direct, indirect, and
structural violence, the dissolution of all injustices and inequali-
ties, where is an educator to begin? How should she proceed?
And how should we respond to the relatively modest hope to
promote the end of, say, the conflict in the Middle East? The all-
encompassing approach, noble as it may be, renders the attempt
to achieve peace in a specific region by educating its specific (future) citizens inconsequential, irrelevant, or—worse—a part of
the violent infrastructure of society.

Similarly, the pedagogic approach's small-scale endeavors to
promote conflict resolution skills fail to carry political significance. In addition, both trends tend to neglect the emotional aspects of peace education.[42] One cannot grow to overcome a specific conflict without learning to address the emotions that sustain
it. The discussion in the next two chapters—on feminist pedagogic contribution (chapter 4) and on forgiveness (in chapter 5)
is aimed, among other things, at responding to this deficiency.

A substantial gap appears to exist between the holistic approach and the pedagogic approach. However, the discussion here reveals a key assumption that plays a problematic role in both of these otherwise different trends. I refer here to the failure or reluctance to differentiate between political conflict (or war) and personal conflict, between state-sponsored violence and personal violence. Although coming from very different backgrounds, the two approaches share a basic shortcoming: a conclusion that is apolitical enough to thwart social implications. Expansive education as an alternative approach to educating for peace shares some of the aims of peace education, but it strives to achieve them through a different path. Peace education that is theoretically sound and practically applicable, as expansive education aims to be, must define itself as a political project. Critical, reflective, engaged citizens can effectively support the alteration of the war culture and help bring about peace. "Conflict resolution training and peace education," Minow reminds us, "risk seeming irrelevant, hypocritical, or distorted if they neglect the larger political frame within which concrete conflicts arise. Yet addressing the larger political frame embroils curriculum in the very disputes it seeks to reshape or transcend."[43] Reshaping or transcending a political conflict cannot occur without an honest critical consideration of the background political circumstances. Feminist and multicultural education by nature of their aim to respond to the realities of social tensions, offer such perspectives, which are examined in the next two chapters.

Feminist Contributions to Expansive Education

IN A TALK AT A JERUSALEM high school a few years ago, a lieutenant general in the Israeli army made a remark that made the next day's headlines: "From time immemorial," he said "men have been warriors, and women—prostitutes." Apparently he was trying, albeit clumsily, to encourage the young men in the audience to volunteer to serve as combat soldiers by referring to the importance of men's service as warriors and the benefits that come along with it, including easy access to sexual favors. His remarks, although prompting some condemning responses, pointed to a common perspective in countries where the public debate is dominated by military and security issues—namely, conservative gender role differentiation, the assertion of men's dominance, and women's servility.

In this chapter I explore a cluster of issues linked by a common focal point: the relations of gender and war. They are examined here in the context of civic education. I start from the widely acknowledged suggestion that militarism and patriarchalism are closely related social phenomena, which together feed undemocratic public inclinations.[1] Among other democratic commitments that are suppressed in times of conflict, gender equality withers in the face of the conservative security state. The more a public domain is preoccupied with security issues, the more it is inclined to move toward conservative conceptions of gender roles. The war situation not only negatively affects women's lives but also affects their social perceptions, making the war an important social and feminist issue of interest.[2]

The argument I make is motivated by the suggestion that the education system has a crucial role in strengthening democracy, in times of peril to security and democracy even more than in peaceful times. The preservation of gender equality is an evident part of this educational responsibility. I begin by examining the links between gender and war, mainly for the purpose of identifying the unique challenges that women face in societies plagued by conflict. The circumstances of conflict and the changes in the conceptualization of citizenship they entail (namely, belligerent citizenship) influence the civic standing of women in various ways. Next I consider feminist theoretical perspectives as well as pedagogical tools that address those unique challenges. The last part of the chapter presents lessons from feminist political thought and pedagogy that can enrich the expansive education approach by offering not only a gendered perspective but also pedagogic tools available for generalization as a response to other social tensions.

WOMEN AND WAR: FRAMING THE CONNECTIONS

On October 31, 2000, the United Nations Security Council unanimously adopted Resolution 1325 on women, peace, and security. It states at the outset that "Resolution 1325 marks the first time the Security Council addressed the disproportionate and unique impact of armed conflict on women, recognized the under-valued and under-utilized contributions women make to conflict prevention, peacekeeping, conflict resolution and peace-building, and stressed the importance of their equal and full participation as active agents in peace and security."[3] The gendered perspective on armed conflict offers numerous viewpoints on the plight and role of women in the context of war. The unique plight of women as victims is the focus of many works: as men fight wars, women are usually the civilians who are hit first and hardest by war and its consequences, such as poverty, expatriation, rape, and destruction.[4] Many authors pursued this line of analysis when considering the relations of gender and war, mostly regarding the fact that men have been the main planners and executors of military violence in the past as a mere contingency or social construction. Another gendered perspective on war is the role women serve in the armed forces, which has been an ongoing debate within feminist circles for the past two decades.[5] A third and less commonly acknowledged aspect, which will be the focus here, is the civic (including educational) consequences of a security-dominated (and thus male-oriented) public sphere. The effects of belligerent citizenship on the public standing of women are often severe, rendering their interests marginal and their actual voices faintly heard in the public realm.

The exploration of the civic consequences of conflict on women's social roles is based on an understanding of both gender and war as social constructions. This suggestion contradicts earlier feminist contentions that women are more peaceful by nature, that femininity is essentially tied to nurturing, or that women are morally superior to men. In a recent book, Joshua Goldstein combines research from a variety of disciplines to claim that gender and war are mutually responsive in their construction.[6] Common Western perceptions of gender and war each grow in the shadow of the other, and the two are inseparable as social entities. Masculinity is defined in the context of war, and war in the context of manifesting masculinity. This mutual influence explicates both the near-total exclusion of women from the combat forces and their near-equal performance as soldiers when they are given the opportunity to fight. The construction of war as a masculine ideal excludes women from fighting in most instances of war, but still women can and do excel in these socially constructed masculine activities when they manage to fight their way into the armed forces.

Similarly, when women serve in military posts, they are not always proven to be more merciful than men. Jean Elshtain offers a detailed account of women and war, describing both the "ferocious few" and the "noncombatant many," as well as the support for various wars by organized and sporadic women's activities.[7] Women cannot be considered peaceful by nature, as is evident from Elshtain's discussion as well as from contemporary examples of women's participation in, and support for, military actions. In Israel the military was forced by the High Court to admit women to combat positions, and consequently a growing number of young women volunteer to serve in various frontline units (although they are still a minority there). Women soldiers have been charged along with their male peers with what feminist philosophers call "gratuitous cruelty,"[8] pointing to the fact that evils associated with masculinity can easily be performed by women in the relevant positions.[9] Even suicide attacks are not a men-only domain anymore; a number of young Palestinian women have perpetrated such attacks against Israeli civilians. Israeli women soldiers have been participating in some of the dehumanizing routines of the occupation, sometimes demonstrating, like their male counterparts, the corruption and cruelty that occupation generates. In the Iraqi prison abuse scandal in Abu Graib, where military wardens seemed to take pleasure in humiliating and torturing their Iraqi prisoners, one of the main perpetrators was a woman. It seems that in past generations, women seldom took part in such acts simply because they were denied the opportunity to do so.

Women apparently share with men the ability to dehumanize the other and to act forcefully when persuaded that this is the right thing to do. Goldstein too, like Elshtain, Cynthia Enloe,[10] and other scholars, offers ample evidence that "when women have found their way into combat, they have generally performed about as well as most men have."[11]

Critics of Goldstein's book found his argument persuasive, to the point of claiming that "the book should lay to rest, once and for all, highly charged debates over the hardwiring of gender traits that associate men with war and women with peace."[12] Goldstein's book is indeed very thorough and offers plenty of evidence to the claim that gender and war are mutually reinforcing social constructions. The conclusion drawn from this claim, however, is highly dependent on one's politics. One critic suggests, following Virginia Woolf's argument in *Three Guineas*, that only equality for women in the public sphere would lead to the obliteration of the war system. Another critic claims that even Goldstein himself misses the important contribution of his findings to "advancing equal opportunity in the military."[13] The relations of gender and war are deeply connected to basic perceptions about what it means to be a man or a woman, what it means to be a social creature, and what is the basis for social relations (care or aggression? desire or hierarchy? reproduction or domination?). This mutual construction of gender and war underlies the fact that some of the civic implications of living in a state of conflict pertain particularly to women. Because women are socially staged in contradiction to both masculinity and war, they are readily marginalized in wartime even when they are represented in the armed forces. Gender-related issues lose standing in the public discourse, as a result of the centrality of security issues. The move toward conservatism, which is a common response to perceived threats, negatively affects the social standing of women. In the educational realm the combination of these two elements creates a shift toward reflecting the culture of war that, among its other disadvantages, offers marginalized portrayals of women.

THE CONSERVATIVE SURGE

In a country in a state of war, security issues tend to surmount most other political matters.[14] References to the acute needs generated by the war permeate discussions on budget, civil rights, and education. The lion's share of these issues is diverted to the private sphere, to be solved (or neglected) there. The further away a question is from the pressing issues of security, the more superficial the public debate about it becomes. Women and many of their interests too are marginalized by the militarized public sphere.

In addition, politicians, the media, and large parts of society tend to be enchanted by the heroism and sacrifice that are generally associated with the military and come to the fore during wartime. In a theoretical discussion it is easier to remember that "war is destruction, pain, separation, gore and savagery as well as strength, courage and heroism."[15] More critical individuals or representatives, in particular in times of a controversial conflict, can focus their attention as well as that of their constituencies on the destruction and pain caused by war. But even in this scenario, the public agenda is overtaken by the responses to war, whether derogatory or laudatory. When a country is immersed in a protracted conflict, the heroic perspective readily becomes a part of the national ethos. The struggle to cope with the destruction and pain that are a constant reality in wartime necessitates a stronger public emphasis on the more compelling aspects of war. The cultivation of this perspective is sometimes portrayed as the duty of the home front in honoring those in combat. The glorification of war, along with the centrality of male-dominated security issues in the public debate, creates a national ethos in which women (like other groups and issues less directly related to the conflict) have little room.

In the post–September 11 United States, the convergence of conservatism and militarism turned into a driving force for

much of the public agenda as well as for some of the administration's policies. One of its most striking intellectual manifestations is William Bennett's *Why We Fight*, an elaborate reconstruction of anger as a driving force for justified male aggression in
the service of patriotism.[16] The conservative public conceptions
of the private sphere and of gender roles are evident in the common depiction of the family in the Israeli debate as well.[17] The
basic presumption concerning the Israeli family is one that
Susan Moller Okin famously criticized: "that families operate
with benignity never expected of . . . the sphere of politics."[18]
The misconception of a strict differentiation between the family
and the sphere of politics is intensified when the latter is preoccupied mostly with war. Compared with the vehement public
sphere of a country under fire, the family seems to glow with
tenderness and care. The public conceptualization of the family
in Israel strives to keep this sentimental portrayal intact. The
conceptual linking of war with masculinity, and of caring for the
home front and the wounded with femininity, generates a public
sphere in which femininity is secondary to masculinity, where
women serve the causes that men actively pursue. Thus, the
family in its classic or conservative form is safeguarded in the
public's mind; within it women are regarded mainly as mothers
and wives. They are expected to keep warm homes for their soldiers—even during more peaceful times, when the men are not
coming home from war but merely from work. In ancient Greece
only citizens who owned land were called upon to protect their
country from invasion, to serve in the military during times of
war. The rationale for this rule was clear to the ancient Greeks
as it is to modern governments: the good soldier is one who has
someone and something to protect. Israeli soldiers, who are not
paid for their years of compulsory service, will be motivated as
long as they believe they are personally protecting their own
homes and families. To promote this attitude, the homes, and
the mothers who are to keep them, are idolized. The American
intensified focus on family values, as was manifested in the 2004
elections, may point to a similar direction. Broadly speaking, a
resemblance can be detected in the general form of conservatism
that is evident in the contemporary public debate in both Israel
and the United States. In the gendered context, in a short and
insightful response to the aftermath of the September 11 attacks,
Iris Marion Young criticizes the benign portrayal of the state as
protector of the vulnerable.[19] Her critical description can readily

be paralleled with the relations of the Israeli populace to its government. In the post–September 11 United States, she claims, the security aspect that characterizes every state took over large parts of the public discourse. The state turned into a security regime: "In the security regime, the state and its officials assume the role of protector toward its citizens, and the citizens become positioned as subordinates, grateful for the protection afforded them." This is an apparently benign description of the masculine role of the state (or of a head of household who assumes the role of the protector). Masculinity here is not portrayed as aggression but rather as chivalry. The citizenry, like the vulnerable members of the household, are thankful for the protection. However, its cost is the unequal relations, the loss of autonomy and voice in decision making, and a broad authoritarian turn that leaves citizens, or women in the household, protected but also subordinate and committed to obedience.

In sum, because gender is a social construct, individuals learn their gendered roles in many ways and through a variety of social agencies. Wartime encourages the depiction of gender as related to a more traditional division of labor. These matters should mostly receive an educational response, broadly construed to include legislation and other public education mechanisms. Unfortunately, the public education system contributes to the perpetuation of gendered social roles; it does so even more rigorously in times of war and in the context of a protracted conflict. It is the education system's responsibility to resume its democratic and civic role by opposing undemocratic social tendencies, one of which is clearly the hierarchical gender differentiation. The next section examines the gendered effects of war on the education system and some critical feminist responses to war in the educational context.

LEARNING TO BE A MAN: EDUCATION, GENDER, AND WAR

The effects of a protracted conflict and a militarized public sphere on the education system are manifold. Chapter 2 recounted some of the ways in which the public education system replicates the mainstream notion of belligerent citizenship. Public pressure and the constitution of the teachers and administrative bodies direct the education system into compliance with the public expectations of creating citizens. In wartime these expectations lean toward unified patriotism, suppression of dissent, and support for the military effort.

The effects of this tendency on women's social standing are evident on the administrative as well as the curricular perspective. One such effect that is uniquely Israeli is the parachuting of retired military officers to lucrative principal positions in the public education system (mainly in high schools). In addition to blocking the paths of promotion to individuals—mostly women—who have devoted their careers to education, this phenomenon also sends a conspicuous public message about social order. Men manage and women are their subordinates, even in professions in which women are a wide majority. Broader gendered consequences of the endorsement of belligerent citizenship by the education system can be found in the curriculum itself. The first and most obvious aspect of the curriculum affected is history studies. The emphasis on military or triumphalistic history and on militarized national narratives of nation building leaves little room for debating other social perspectives or presenting historical contributions of women. This problem, evident in more tranquil countries as well, worsens when a protracted conflict takes its toll on the curricular emphases. The presentation of an occasional woman who was allowed to serve and excelled, volunteered to do crucial paramilitary work, or was a devoted nurse, only serves to highlight the absence of women from the curriculum and from the militarized version of national history.

Another problematic effect of belligerent citizenship on schools from the gendered perspective is the differentiated socialization of men and women. In Israel, a democracy that mandates service to both men and women, the effects of the militarized culture on public schooling are mostly evident in the military-oriented socialization of boys and girls. Boys and girls anticipate a different future, with many boys and few girls aspiring from a very young age to serve in combat positions. A considerable part of youth socialization toward their roles is correspondingly split.

In a democratic society that does not practice universal draft and has a narrower gender differentiation in military roles, like the United States, the effects of the military civic socialization

83

of young people are more subtle. The gendered culture of war, however, has its differentiated effect on young men and women.[20] Belligerent citizenship relies on a positive conception of war as a necessity, even a virtue, of political action. Both Israel's and the contemporary United States' common depiction of the conflicts in which they are engaged is one that was forced upon them. The necessity of going to war, however, turns into a virtue from the civic perspective, with expressions of support for the causes of war viewed as manifestations of a unified form of patriotism, which involves an endorsement of the gendered characterization of war. The heroism being heralded is mostly a masculine one, with an occasional heroine (like the mythic aspects of the Jessica Lynch story during the Iraq war) whose story nourishes the masculine glory of the fight. This view of civic virtue as militaristic and thus masculine carries belligerent qualities over into the public conception of the Good Citizen, which grows to accommodate the combat soldier as the embodiment of good citizenship (along with other visions of good citizenship, but still with significant weight). This conceptualization, along with the reorganization of notions of patriotism and national identity, has an impact on schools almost immediately after the beginning of an armed conflict, through ad hoc lesson plans as well as "hidden curricula" materials.[21] Later on it infiltrates the public education system through history books, civic studies curricula, and other standardized forms of learning.

The feminist critique of the education system in times of a protracted conflict thus points out the portrayal of women as occupying traditional roles, and the emphasis on men's heroism, as main aspects that require attention. What constructive suggestions can be found in feminist literature from which a response can be developed? Feminist pedagogical contributions to peace education offer an outline for an answer.

Women as Peacemakers? An Educational Perspective

The feminist literature has long suggested that women's experiences—specifically mothers' experiences—offer a productive basis for a philosophy of peace. Much as patriarchalism and war seem to have significant relations of mutual reinforcement, so do feminism—or femininity, or motherhood, or simply women—and peace.[22]

The opposition of care and justice—and thus of women's and men's moral perspectives—serves as a background for various feminist political theories, "maternal thinking" perhaps most prominent among them. Since Sara Ruddick's groundbreaking book,[23] the practice of motherhood has been considered by many feminist philosophers and educators as a benchmark of peacemaking politics. According to Ruddick, mothers are concerned with preserving the life of the child, fostering her growth, and training her for social acceptability. They use analytical as well as emotional work toward these goals and toward overcoming violence, including their own. Under this description, motherhood provides tools for a peaceful resolution of conflicts in both personal and political contexts. Ruddick's account of maternal work and its significance to peace politics derives much of its force from reference to the masculinity of war and of women's peacefulness. She too regards both as social constructions: in a paraphrase of Simone de Beauvoir's words, she says, "A boy is not born, but rather becomes, a soldier."[24] Ruddick was not the first to philosophically examine the connection between women's lives and peace. Back in 1938 Virginia Woolf devoted her essay *Three Guineas* to the exploration of the relations between the two, with a substantial discussion of related educational matters. Woolf regards the poverty of women, and their lack of formal education in her time, as one of the causes for the prevalence of war. She calls for more and better education for women, suggesting that their inclusion in the public world of politics will result in more peaceful policies.

These perspectives, though revolutionary for their times and providing important insight into the research of gender, are the context of criticism for feminist and other authors who resist the direct association of an individual's gender with her/his moral affiliation. Gender and morality (much like the narrower relations of gender and war) mutually construct each other; various characteristics can be attributed to one gender more than the other, but the correlation should be interpreted in social construction terms rather than as essential components of each gender. Contrary to Woolf's intuition, the inclusion of women in the public and political sphere is not perceived today as promoting peace (although it is a valuable goal notwithstanding). Contrary to Ruddick, many contemporary authors justifiably describe motherhood in more complex terms, regarding it more substantially as constructed by cultural and social expectations, and as less supportive of exclusively peaceful relations, both personal and sociopolitical.

If indeed women do not have essential moral perspectives that offer an alternative to the dominant male morality—if they (we) do not harbor a tendency to peaceful social relations, whether as women or as mothers, why is it still worth discussing education and war in a feminist context? What is the relevance of the feminist educational perspective to the debate about citizenship and war, and why is it productive to suggest, as I do, that feminist pedagogical practices should be integrated into a broader conception of civic education in wartime, such as the expansive education approach?

Women have a unique contribution to make in the field of education generally, and peace education specifically, because of two factors: first, the burden that war places on women both in reality and in social perception; and second, their disproportional contribution to the education of children—both their own children as mothers and other people's children, as teachers. The socialization of children into their role as citizens, family members, and public actors has been the role of women for many generations, in their capacity as caregivers at home and by their function as an overwhelming majority among educators in recent generations. Despite this fact, various masculinist tendencies are expressed in the formal education system, even in peaceful times; consequently, some trends in feminist theory have suggested pedagogical ways to incorporate feminist insights into the structure and content of the education system. I will not discuss here the entire breadth of insights that are derived from care ethics, but will focus on those that are most applicable to civic education in wartime.[25] As I suggested, male-dominated tendencies in the public sphere generally, and in public education specifically, surge during wartime. Educators working in this context should be aware that, among other impacts of war on the education system, the security-dominated public sphere can push the curriculum and other educational practices in the direction of less recognition, space, and voice for women. Feminist pedagogy can aid in constructing a nuanced response to this challenge.

Feminist pedagogy offers guidelines to education for positive recognition of the gendered, racial, ethnic, and national "other."

It provides a tactic and tools for overcoming oppression and expanding the social sphere to include a diverse citizenry. As such, it offers an invaluable instrument for education in wartime. Expansive education, in its effort to oppose the attenuating public sphere, can use lessons drawn from feminist pedagogies, lessons that were often developed through struggle against narrow social conceptions that failed to accommodate women's perspectives.

The most influential and effective feminist perspective on education was offered by bell hooks: "Talk back."[26] This simple phrase symbolizes the main cause of feminist as well as other radical and critical trends of education. The critical response to the social mainstream, both by analysis and by political activism, is the crux of any educational approach that trusts education to be an anchor for social change. Engaged pedagogy is a term used by hooks to describe a holistic approach to teaching and learning. It values students' and teachers' expressions and risk taking, recognizing and challenging power issues. As a student of Paulo Freire, hooks values the mutual work of student and teacher in opposing the social mainstream.

Feminist theory often regards education as a crucial step on the road to gender equality (however that notion is conceived). Beyond demands for equal access to educational resources, which are less consequential to the discussion on education in wartime, feminist theory can contribute other pragmatic tools to the educational effort to achieve peace. When looking for ways to teach peace and democracy against a rising tide of unifying patriotism and erosion of democratic commitments, educators will find helpful the forms of resistance suggested by feminist pedagogy.

Nonviolence

Contrary to Just War theorists, Sara Ruddick claims that she is "not preoccupied with the question, When, if ever, is it right to kill?" Rather she "seeks to expose the multiple costs of violence and to disrupt the plans of those who organize it."[27] Ruddick construes feminist peace politics as a subversive activity that is wary of organized violence, discloses hidden violence, and invents strategies and ideals of nonviolence.

Significant feminist scholarly work has been devoted to teaching strategies for defying violence and affirming peacefulness. Some authors, such as Brock-Utne and Reardon, investigate the peace education realm through a gendered lens; Brock-Utne's broad definition of war as any situation involving the breach of human rights, inequality, poverty, and public and personal violence leads her to the claim that "peace starts in the minds of women."[28] Other authors offer pedagogical tools that can enhance skills and attitudes necessary for building a peaceful class climate or a peaceful community. Nel Noddings suggests a pedagogy of care that is designed to encourage humane and cooperative rather than competitive and aggressive interaction in school (and beyond).[29] Still other authors, employing a gender-sensitive approach,[30] provide tools for dealing with the structural violence of gender oppression as well as the practical violence in the form of harassment or physical attacks against women within and outside the educational realm. These feminist tools combine cognitive and emotional perspectives toward the goal of learning new ways of perceiving the "other" as well as nonviolent modes of expressing one's views. Although a description of all those tools is beyond the scope of this work, it is worth mentioning their common structure, which they share with the expansive education approach. The feminist struggle against the exclusion of women that is inherent to traditional social perceptions is pursued by peaceful means and as part of an attempt not to conquer social constructions but to expand them so that they include further perspectives. The message of nonviolence is crucial in itself in a public realm that is enchanted by the heroic perception of war and thus can offer a key contribution to expansive education.

Recognition

Feminist literature has long claimed that women are commonly identified as the "other" within the social order. Feminist theorists provide strategies for learning to overcome alienation, to recognize and respect the "other," and to create common grounds beyond differences. One such tool for generating and reinforcing recognition is through dialogue, which is a tool employed by various radical, postcolonial, antiracist, and post-structural pedagogies. Generating recognition through establishing a meaningful dialogue among teachers and students, and within a diverse group of students, is a means to overcoming stereotypes and animosity.[31] The recognition of difference is a valuable tool for beginning to consider different needs and interests for policy purposes as well as for learning to respect other perspectives and values. The recognition of difference is a good in itself, as well as a tool for the purpose of diversifying the voices heard in public. A broader array of voices in the public realm works against the wartime focus of public debate on security issues; it also serves to empower members of groups, including women, that otherwise are discouraged from representing their perspectives.

RESISTANCE

Feminist pedagogy emphasizes the oppositional ways of educating against widespread social perceptions. Where women are conceived of as vulnerable, voiceless, or unworthy, education can empower them, give them voice, and foster their differences and similarities in ways that can change their self- and social perception. Resisting widely held social prejudices and opposing an oppressive social mainstream have been key goals of feminist pedagogy for decades. By using methods such as questioning basic assumptions, presenting students with unconventional role models, and encouraging them to think critically about the construction and content of their social beliefs, feminists have managed to push forward the social recognition of women as equal members of society.

This educational process needs to engage both the cognitive critical abilities of students and teachers and their emotional affinity. Feminist pedagogy at its best challenges a multiplicity of widely accepted dichotomies, including the cognition/emotion one. Hence, a feminist pedagogy offers educational tools that engage students' feelings, beliefs, and knowledge with a critical consideration of current social practices. Much like peace pedagogies at their best, the process of change and growth that takes place through feminist pedagogy respectfully involves the individual in all her complexity. Fear, hate, and misconceptions must be present in the classroom, acknowledged and dealt with rather than flatly rejected. For students to be able to reconceptualize notions of gender, nationalism, or patriotic commitments (as well as of race, class, and other social matters), their initial perception of these must be recognized in class. This learning process thus is a mutual one, involving the teacher who has to respond to the students' conceptual world and the students who may learn to overcome misconceptions and grow to think about themselves and others in fresh, broader ways.[32] This approach can readily be adapted to expansive education and to classrooms engaged in civic education for peace.

Positive Self-Conception

Feminist pedagogy highlights the positionality of learners and instructors and engages them in a quest for emancipation.[33] As in the case of dialogical pedagogy from the Freire school, which informs trends in feminist pedagogy, this emancipation is manifested through strengthening the positive self-conception of the learners. The empowerment of learners, a distinctive aim of all radical pedagogies, expresses itself in the case of feminist pedagogy also in the form of creating a positive conception of the future self. Nel Noddings notes that the teacher must offer confirmation to the student by attributing to her the most positive motives possible; by this and other ways she can support the student's confidence and help her build a conception of herself as a positive person in the present and in the future.

Helping a student establish a positive future self-conception is arguably the most important contribution that a teacher can have in a student's life. Being able to imagine oneself as a positive person and anticipating a desirable future is an essential component for overcoming present-time difficulties, peer pressures, self-doubts, and actual failure. How this goal can be achieved is a question that hardly has a simple answer, and it is beyond the scope of the present work to discuss the many aspects of personal and social affirmation, empowerment, and expectation that make an environment suitable for developing such self-conception. This notion is stressed here because it carries much significance to the question at hand, namely the feminist educational and pedagogic ways of promoting peace. Adapting this tool for expansive education purposes requires expanding it to the social arena. A main aim of civic education for peace is to enable the formation of a positive vision of the future, a positive communal self-conception that incorporates the role of the nation in the region and world. Regarding oneself as an American, Palestinian, Iraqi, or Israeli and finding a nonmilitaristic form of pride in this identification can contribute to the emergence of an expanded and inclusive patriotism that does not rely solely on belligerent forms of nationalism. Envisioning a different future for the country one identifies with depends on a host of variables, some of which can be addressed in the school setting. Students get their information from the news and other media, from possible engagement with the political world, from their family members and their communities. Schools, however, can offer a perspective that goes beyond what many children may learn in these and other settings. Schools can work with the students, engaging their critical capacities, emotions, and imagination, to envision alternative possible futures other than the grim or triumphalist ones that a country engaged in a protracted conflict tends to generate.

These approaches and tools are of immense importance to civic education in wartime and toward peace. They can serve the goal of overcoming past differences and learning to live alongside the former adversary as neighbor or fellow citizen; of preserving democratic values and attitudes despite belligerent citizenship; as well as supporting the nation itself in the transition toward peace, which is a demanding and often divisive project.

To summarize, the relations between gender and peace are multilayered. First, the culture of war and militarism is a patriarchal culture; chauvinism and male chauvinism go hand in hand. Although many women support war in various ways, they are hit hard by its consequences, both practically and perceptually. Women's vulnerability to war as well as to the war culture puts them in a unique position to oppose the social circumstances created by a protracted conflict. "Obedience is the handmaid of war, resistance the prerequisite of peace."[34] Being able to resist the temptation of unity and solidarity offered by the belligerent form

Multicultural Education:
Acknowledgment and Forgiveness

> Central to modern expectations, and modern
> ethical feeling, is the conviction that war is an
> aberration, if an unstoppable one. That peace is
> the norm, if an unattainable one. This, of
> course, is not the way war has been regarded
> throughout history. War has been the norm and
> peace the exception.
> —Susan Sontag, *Regarding the Pain of Others*

THE COMPLEX PROCESS of responding to conflict while preserving
democratic inclinations can benefit from drawing on multicultural curricula and theoretical approaches. The mission of expansive education is best described as educationally responding
to conflict while continually supporting the effort to create democratic citizens. Multicultural education is best described as the
mission to educationally respond to social conflicts, tensions,
and differences while creating democratic citizens. The contextual differences—the fact that multicultural education does not
commonly respond to armed conflict but rather to social tensions, and the fact that the groups involved in the conflict are in
one case typically separate along national lines and in the other
case comembers of the same society—do not undermine the similarities between the two approaches. In particular these differences should not divert our attention from the potential mutual
enrichment. This chapter will focus on two issues within the vast
literature on multicultural education that are most promising for
programs of civic education for peace: acknowledgment and forgiveness. These two concepts are the most helpful ones for
expansive education because they are the main relational aspects of multicultural education. The identity-related aspects of
multicultural education are of less help here because expansive

education is aimed at working with (and toward) strengthening notions of shared fate to supplement the moral reality of nationalism as perceived identity. Both acknowledgment and forgiveness can inform a democratic conception of citizenship as shared fate, which support the key aspects of expansive education, namely, peace building and democracy.

MULTICULTURALISM AND EXPANSIVE EDUCATION: FRAMING THE CONNECTIONS

The sociopolitical theory of multiculturalism combines philosophical accounts of the just society, with considerations of political necessities in actual societies. Multicultural approaches are broadly aimed at reconciling the twin aims of unity and diversity. Expansive education is similarly focused on finding room for diversity without forgoing the unity of society, which is indispensable for endurance in wartime. A balanced approach to expansive education can thus benefit from the theoretical insights and practical tools offered by scholars of multiculturalism. Education serves as a focal point in multicultural thought, with claims on the formal system varying from recognition to cultural segregation. Multiculturalists expect public recognition of cultural difference, representation of diverse groups and their perspectives in the public sphere, and other manifestations of moral and civic equality of diverse social groups. Developing through these venues the skills to mediate differences between rival social groups within a given nation is an educational process that could be adapted to the context of mediating national animosities.

Thus, multicultural approaches and tools can be applicable to the processes of peace building through civic education, of overcoming the culture of war through investing in education for democracy. Expansive education shares with multiculturalism one of its most valued stated goals, namely, to know and respect the "other." For multiculturalism, the "other" usually consists of other citizens in the same state, members of the same society. The more specific definition of the "other" varies widely from place to place, even within the same country. In Philadelphia or

New York City, black and white residents of the same neighborhood may perceive the "other" in terms of race; in southern Arizona the "other" is perceived along the lines of white/Mexican/Latino. In the Israeli/Palestinian context, the "other" is defined by nationality, religion, and ethnic origins. These differences are not mere contingencies but fundamental components of multicultural claims within the educational and political arenas. A major principle of multiculturalism is its contextuality, its focus on the concrete "other" with all its complexity. Multiculturalism is meant to offer an opportunity to meet the concrete others and learn about their specificities as well as recognize common humanity beyond differences: "[A]ccording to one especially compelling formulation, [multiculturalism] is the radical idea that people in other cultures, foreign and domestic, are human beings, too."[1]

This formulation draws attention to those aspects of multiculturalism that can most benefit the aims of expansive education. Multiculturalism uses educational tools to overcome the different manifestations of comparable social phenomena like hatred and dehumanization. Ignoring our shared humanity to hide behind essentialist group descriptions that provide a sense of unity through the rejection of the "other" is a phenomenon that occurs across national groups and cultural lines. This can hint to the possibility of applying related educational strategies—tools that were developed in the multicultural literature can be shared between the two philosophical-political projects. Learning to bridge rifts, to overcome hatred, to take the other's perspective, to recognize other historical narratives are all potential parts of both multicultural and expansive education. In both cases they must be socially and culturally contextualized if they are to remain relevant and responsive. It is thus the relational aspect of multicultural education that can be most helpful for the project of sustaining democracy while responding constructively to the challenges of belligerent citizenship.

I now turn to explore the two relational aspects of multicultural thought that are most important to consider in the context of war and thus are most adaptable to the needs of expansive education. The first is acknowledgment, or the reconceptualization of the "other" through overcoming stereotypes and learning to accept differing perspectives on salient social matters. The second is forgiveness, with the political, social, and educational processes that can nourish it until it surmounts blame and hatred. The analysis and pedagogical uses of acknowledgment in multicultural education are available for implementation in an expansive education curriculum (following some changes in focus); the ensuing pedagogical model of forgiveness needs to be restructured in order to be productively applied to the social and educational circumstances of civic education for peace during wartime.

On Acknowledging Past Wrongs

Multicultural education evolved as a response to charges of social injustice against minority subgroups. Broadly speaking, it offers two lines of argumentation: the first is based on a demand for toleration, which entails a passive respect for other cultures and the freedom to practice or express them privately; the other line of argument focuses on the need for recognition, or the public acceptance (or celebration) of publicly expressed differences. The demand for recognition is often viewed as exclusive to that of tolerance. Amy Gutmann puts it this way: "Either citizens should tolerate their cultural differences by privatizing them, or they should respect their cultural differences by publicly recognizing them."[2]

Michael Walzer offers a thorough defense of the argument for toleration in the political arena.[3] At its core, it is a demand for tolerance, which albeit political, relegates the relevant differences among groups outside the public sphere, to be practiced there and tolerated by the general public as private idiosyncrasies. Religious tolerance is based on the claim that belief is a personal matter, that whatever one chooses to believe or however she chooses to worship cannot be (and should not be) communicated in publicly justifiable terms and should not be evaluated by others who do not share her beliefs. Cultural tolerance is largely based on the similar claim that a group's cultural heritage, traditions, beliefs, and symbols are not open to analysis or evaluation by outsiders. The argument is in essence one that maintains the judgment of cultural practices within the border of the cultural community. This is the strength of the tolerance argument, and this is where it fails to be applicable to the field of international reconciliation, particularly to the effort of reconciliation and the overcoming of past and present conflicts through education: describing the differences between adversary national groups as private or internal to each group demonstrates a failure to overcome the consequences of those differences to international or intergroup relations. Whether a conflict between nations (or other groups) results from territorial differences, cultural or racial clashes, religious charges, or any combination of these factors, relegating them to the intragroup realm does nothing to solve the issue.[4]

The multicultural argument for recognition and acknowledgment is more promising for the purposes of expansive education. It centers on the claim for public recognition of relevant differences among groups, including the benefits that complement such recognition. For many the demand for recognition is accompanied by an equally strong claim for acknowledgment of past wrongs. Social conflict or structural discrimination can affect the education system in ways similar to those of national conflict and other military struggles. The perceived sensitivity of the topic, the social tensions surrounding it or its controversialism in the public sphere, impels the education system to be wary of directly addressing it. As it shies away from addressing the controversial issues, the education system may inadvertently replicate the tensions and stereotypes that nourish them. Minority groups in society, often burdened with past wrongs and present discrimination, regularly face a further burden in the form of a society that knows little about their culture, life conditions, and relational background. The basic reason for demanding recognition—for introducing all members of society to the unique features of subgroups with whom they share the public space—is that "our identity is partly shaped by recognition or its absence, often by *mis*recognition of others."[5] As Charles Taylor observes, social recognition is central to the individual's identity and self-worth, and misrecognition can gravely damage both. In addition, misrecognition or the absence of recognition undermines the project of constituting citizenship as shared fate.

In this sense, the claims of multicultural education are broader than those of expansive education. In the latter case, the identities of the adversarial sides may be affected by the conflict (particularly if it is a protracted conflict). Thus, Palestinians can define their identity (at least partially) by their opposition to the Israeli occupation, Bosnians can self-identify through their distinctiveness from Serbs, and so on. Still there is a significant distinction from the context in which multiculturalism operates: the distinctiveness is based on self-identification, not on misrecognition by the other. The other group is significant as an "other" but it less fundamentally serves as the main reference point that provides a description of the group to its members as sharing a communal fate.

Thus, the uses of recognition and acknowledgment in multicultural education are related to the purpose of establishing a just public sphere and an environment in which members of all subgroups may learn and develop; in expansive education they are related to the preservation of just, democratic inclinations. The multicultural demand for cultural recognition, and for the acknowledgment of past wrongs, is evident in the bulk of literature pertaining to Native Americans and African Americans, aboriginal cultures, and Canadian First Nations.[6] Central to such recognition is the demand for acknowledgment of past relations of groups within society, including ways they wronged each other and the consequences of these wrongs in their present relative conditions. This is far from claiming that what is required is an economy of "an eye for an eye." Looking for ways to understand the past does not ideally entail calculations of blame and contestation on the role of the victim. This in fact may lead to sustaining conflict rather than overcoming its consequences. Neither does it mean that we need to vindicate historical actions in order for a different future to evolve. A racially just American society cannot be expected to first punish all those responsible for or those who profited from slavery, and not only because it is a matter of the past. For Israelis and Palestinians to rebuild the Middle East as a peaceful region, there can be no realistic expectation to calculate all the various ways in which each side victimized, terrorized, or oppressed the other. What the requirement for acknowledgment does mean is that all sides need to learn to look at their common history and their respective current conditions from a more complex perspective than is usually available to them for the purpose of advancing both peace and democracy. In a careful analysis of acknowledgment as a political prerequisite for amending past wrongs, Trudy Govier asserts that acknowledgment "is a necessary condition of willingness to make restitution and commit to positive change."[7] Contrasting acknowledgment to deception and self-deception, Govier demonstrates how getting over denial and focusing our attention on (past and present) deficiencies constitutes a first step on the road to forgiveness. Education is the proper institution to undertake this task, for it is the first formal institution that all (future) citizens encounter. As such it has a potential influence on all individuals, as well as a crucial declaratory role in the social and political life of the community.

Choosing to acknowledge rather than deny past wrongs is a crucial step in the process of overcoming mutual hostilities, for both perpetrator and victim. This was the rationale of the Truth and Reconciliation Commission (TRC) in South Africa and of similar projects in other countries. The South African commission assumed that reconciliation interests should override those of retributive justice, and so the public acknowledgment of atrocities was preferred over that of prosecuting offenders from the past apartheid regime.[8] "Acknowledgement is knowledge accompanied by a kind of marking, spelling out or admitting as significantly related to oneself something that is known," says Govier.[9] One fundamental way of publicly expressing acknowledgment is the studying of past wrongs in state-sponsored public schools.

EDUCATION AND ACKNOWLEDGMENT: JUSTIFYING REVERSE PATRIOTISM

Wartime generates a narrow notion of patriotism, which often tends to be reflected in the educational arena, along with a denial of the other side to the conflict. Focusing mainly on the nationalist version of the historic narrative, presenting an inhumane description of the enemy's actions, focusing on "our" side as a victim and the other as a ruthless offender or on triumphalistic presentations of history—all serve the unreflective aims of education in wartime, which compromise the study of history, perpetuate injustices inflicted on the adversary group, and undermine critical thinking, an essential part of democratic education.[10] Acknowledgment is a key aspect of multicultural education that can help respond in constructive way to the exclusive, uncritical forms of belligerent patriotism by generating what I call reverse patriotism.

Multicultural education and expansive education share the need to overcome a history of injustice and harm and to create a comparable vision of a positive future. However, multicultural education must confront the need to create a shared history from the narratives of various groups, whereas expansive education needs to focus more on acknowledgment as a precondition for preserving democratic attitudes. Multicultural history should be owned and accepted by all sides, in order for them to be able to participate in a common future.[11] James Banks, one of the pioneers of multicultural education, was among the first scholars to examine schools as social systems within a multicultural context.[12] According to Banks, in order to maintain a "multicultural school environment," all aspects of the school must be examined and transformed, including policies, teachers' attitudes and instructional materials, assessment methods, counseling, and teaching styles.[13] These aspects should be transformed to reflect the variety of cultures represented in the larger society in which the school operates. The peace aspect of expansive education requires less than that—it requires recognition of the other's perspective of history, but it allows the former adversaries to hold on to their separate, often conflicting versions of the conflict (and other aspects of their histories). The compatibility of historical narratives between former enemies is less crucial for achieving peace and democracy, although it is essential that the portrayal of the conflict and the adversary are humane and reflective rather than self-congratulatory or demeaning. Hence, the main purpose of acknowledgment within expansive education is that of enhancing peaceful rather than belligerent tendencies while acknowledging the social need for unity and endurance and preserving democratic attitudes and skills. The inclusion of acknowledgment in the curriculum as well as the pedagogical work is required in order to enhance the recognition of the (former) enemy, to allow for a culture of peace to be generated, and most important, to maintain a complex moral view of one's own group and the adversary group(s). This moral complexity is the baseline of an evolving democratic perspective on the conflict, which supports the balancing of belligerent tendencies with an acknowledgment of the other's humanity. Multiculturalism reminds us of the need to acknowledge past wrongs, to recognize differences of groups within society in their multiplicities, and to learn to forgive. All these are important potential contributions to the process of peace building in general and expansive education in particular. Most important, multiculturalism stresses the significance of revising the educational perspective comprehensively, not merely by adding a unit to the curriculum or introducing one disconnected feature into the school day (or year). In one of the most careful analyses of the conditions of multiculturalism, Bhikhu Parekh expresses mistrust in the blunt attempt to incorporate a host of "other perspectives" into the curriculum. This critique is similar to the one against the tendency of early feminist responses to "add women and stir." For Parekh, a meaningful multicultural curriculum must conform to two conditions. "First, it should not be unduly narrow."[14] Monocultural education, much like belligerent civic education, is confined to presenting students with a narrow perspective of history and culture in the hope of enlisting them to the cohorts of supporters of the nation. A major goal of a multicultural education is thus the expansion of the students' understanding of their group's and nation's history, through connecting it with the histories of the region and the world. In this multicultural education converges with expansive education based on citizenship as shared fate. Both acknowledge the necessity of understanding the connectedness of individuals who share the same fate by virtue of their group membership. Acknowledging the multiplicity of cultures and histories that make up the nation is an inevitable component of a multicultural curriculum. Similarly, learning to understand a nation's place in the history and current affairs of the region and the world is a necessary part of expansive education. As Parekh notes, expanding the students' horizons and including various perspectives of history and other curricular subjects does not have to amount to fostering a relativistic notion of history or morals. It does not mean that the local, ethnic, or national culture and history must be abandoned in favor of a superficial curriculum that aims to cover everything in the world. The limitation of time makes it necessary to choose what to teach and what to put aside, in the hope that the students' curiosity and learning skills will help them get to some of the neglected knowledge later in life. It is reasonable for students to have more interest in what is closer to home, and there is reason to teach students more about their own culture and history and that of their fellow students and citizens. For the purposes of both multicultural education and expansive education, the study of local cultures and histories serves the aims of recognition. When properly addressed, the study of local histories, of the nation in its relations to subgroups and to other nations, can serve also as a springboard for acknowledging both differences and past wrongs.

The second condition Parekh mentions for a multicultural curriculum has to do with pedagogy. "It is not enough to broaden the curriculum," he says, with different religions, historical perspectives, or cultures. "One should also bring them into a fruitful dialogue."[15] Dialogue is a pedagogic tool, the importance of which for civic learning, and particularly expansive education, cannot be overstated.[16] By generating dialogue in the classroom between teacher and students, between cultures, between political perspectives, educators serve key aims of multiculturalism, namely, acknowledgment and empowerment. They simultaneously serve a fundamental aim of expansive education: expanding the limits of acceptable opinions and arguing for a variety of perspectives. Creating a cultural and national dialogue in schools is an important step on the road to creating a political dialogue. Such dialogue can promote and sustain peaceful relations both socially and politically. Engaged in classroom debate and dialogue, students can develop an informed perspective about various matters and assess them in light of other possible views on the subject. They can learn to grasp the contextuality of historical truths. Ideally, they can learn to appreciate the complexity of analyzing historical, political, and social circumstances. Even without subscribing to a relativist view of society and history, they can, in the context of an international conflict, learn to appreciate the other side's perspective, going beyond the dehumanization of the other.

Thus acknowledgment, when introduced into the curriculum and pedagogy in a comprehensive way, allows for reversing the patriotic tendencies of the (history, civics, and other) curricula. "Reverse" here does not point to the annulment or invalidation of existing patriotic feelings, as expressed by belligerent citizenship. Rather it means "contrary" or "divergent"—drawing attention to the expansion of the given meaning of the notion "patriotism." The introduction of acknowledgment allows for such reversing because it still focuses on the nation but not solely through the mythic stories of heroism and nation building or through a triumphalistic narration of history. Rather it encourages the students and teachers to understand and identify with their nation (or group) with its complex history, to own it, and thus to be willing to amend what needs to be amended. Reversing the trend of patriotism does not mean rejecting it but rather supplementing the patriotic teachings with a more complex view of the relational history of the nation. This reverse patriotism is an aspect of citizenship as shared fate, for it expands the limits of the national group to include denied or silenced perspectives and groups, as well as aspects of history. It thus supports the evolvement of a shared vision of the nation that is more inclusive and thus more democratic.

All these aspects of acknowledgment—bringing cultures and historical perspectives into a fruitful dialogue, recognizing the other's humanity, expanding by reversing patriotic teaching—can serve as a first step in the long journey into forgiveness. Positively and consciously reconstructing collective memories to make them more receptive to peaceful relations is a process that can face many challenges. Undertaking this task in schools requires a mindful restructuring of the curriculum and methods of teaching. The renewed curriculum, expanded to include a variety of perspectives, can support the generation of a constructive dialogue. To pave the road for both peace and democracy, forgiveness must follow the acknowledgment of past wrongs to allow all parties to begin envisioning a positive common future.

FORGIVENESS AS AN EDUCATIONAL GOAL

Forgiveness is the next step after the acknowledgment of past wrongs, if one can create the proper conditions that enable it. Since the very idea of forgiveness presupposes an identification of the other as guilty, this other must also acknowledge his guilt (or wrongdoing) in order for the forgiveness to reverberate in the political sphere. Some contemporary authors go as far as asserting that a public acknowledgment of violence, oppression, or atrocities accompanied by an appropriate apology can establish the sole basis necessary for the evasion of war.[17]

An important part of the civic conditions for forgiveness can, again, be attained in schools. The notion of forgiveness as a pedagogic practice and as a moral educational goal was introduced into educational theory mostly by multicultural education theorists seeking ways to overcome past wrongs and work toward the establishment of a just common society. The moral education field has also regained interest in the concept of forgiveness in recent years.[18] Possibly prompted by a renewed interest in war and ethnic conflict, scholars have been debating various types of forgiveness and modes of teaching them in schools. Moral philosophers too are debating epistemological and ethical aspects of forgiveness.[19]

Contemporary educational and moral literature offers three basic models of forgiveness. Well-known and most radical among them is the one offered by Jacques Derrida. Much like educational and other literature on the issue, it relies heavily on religious traditions: "As enigmatic as the concept of forgiveness remains," Derrida writes, "it is the case that the scene, the figure, the language which one tries to adapt to it belong to a religious heritage (let's call it Abrahamic, in order to bring together Judaism, the Christianities, and the Islams)."[20] Derrida suggests that forgiveness is an act that is entirely at the hands and heart of the victim, and is given unconditionally and without expectation of return. Forgiving the unforgivable is the only true act of forgiveness, for "[i]f one is only prepared to forgive what appears forgivable, what the church calls 'venial sin,' then the very idea of forgiveness would disappear."[21] Thus, forgiveness at its purest form cannot entail any expectations of restitution, repentance, or compensation. This is a very religious—more specifically, a very Christian—notion of forgiveness, based on a leap of faith as its true expression. It corresponds with earlier discussions, most notably Hannah Arendt's, of forgiveness as a singular and unworldly act, which is strictly intimate and relates (to use Levinas's notion) to the "face" of the other.[22] A moving manifestation of this form of unconditional forgiveness, generated solely by the emotions and beliefs of the victim rather than by the actions of the "sinner" or wrongdoer, was seen in the trial of Henry Hays in 1981, a member of the Ku Klux Klan who was found guilty of lynching a black teenage boy. Before his verdict was read in the courtroom, he turned to the victim's mother and asked if she could ever forgive him. Quietly, she replied, "I have already forgiven you."[23]

This type of forgiveness, albeit noble, bears little relevance beyond the religious and interpersonal context. Intergroup and international relations seem to require further steps beyond a leap of faith and the declaration of forgiveness to establish peaceful relations between former adversaries. Hence, despite the moral appeal of this model, many authors acknowledge that other models should be considered for political-educational purposes. Derrida himself states that this pure form of forgiveness does not relate to the political process of reconciliation. Consequently, many discussions of forgiveness part with the Derrida model in establishing some link between justice and forgiveness. Restitution and the restoration of justice can be a prelude to a formal act of forgiveness. Forgiveness, if it is to be politicized, cannot be summarized as unworldly (as Derrida suggests) or entirely intimate (as Arendt suggests, echoing Levinas). The demand to do justice, by punishing the offender or by compensating the victim, can be presented by the victim as a precondition to granting her forgiveness, which thus turns into a sociopolitical act. More broadly, the acknowledgment of injustice in past relations or actions is a necessary condition for ensuring that they do not occur again after forgiveness was granted. This link between justice and forgiveness is evident in two widely debated models of forgiveness, the "strict model" and the "relaxed model."

The strict view of forgiveness presupposes the wrongdoer's repentance and/or just punishment and proclaims the granting of forgiveness as the victim's moral or religious duty. Hence, if the offender repents the wrong he did (with or without being punished, by God or man) and asks for forgiveness, its granting ensues promptly. In a position spurred by the strict model, Tara Smith argues that forgiveness is not a virtue but rather a moral duty of the victim, which is directly derivative of a claim of justice. Hence, for justice to be served, the victim must forgive the offender when the appropriate conditions are fulfilled; otherwise he himself becomes a wrongdoer, an obstacle to justice.[24] This view is rightly criticized as too formal or rigid and too dependent on an exchange economy.

The Derrida model and the strict and religious views are thus only marginally relevant to education in the context of group or national conflict. Waiving demands for justice and describing forgiveness as a moral duty of the harmed side(s) can hardly be constructively implemented to this setting.

The relaxed view is sometimes described as the "no problem" model of forgiveness.[25] This is the model most commonly used in educational settings, in particular in the education of young children. Under this model, children should learn to forgive easily and with no demand for punishment or compensations for harms done to them. We should teach children to forgive because "it is a matter, on the one side, of encouraging a willingness to apologise and make amends (if possible) combined, on the other, with a generous acceptance of people who have caused one hurt."[26] Forgiveness here is not precisely a duty; it is more of a social nicety. One's obligation to forgive is not a moral requirement but rather a social imperative or expectation, deriving from norms of politeness. White claims that this approach to forgiveness is a "generous-spirited attitude between equals" which is "well-suited to a liberal democratic multi-ethnic society."[27] However, equality between the two sides is not always expressed in group conflict, and merely assuming it for the sake of constituting a forgiving attitude does not establish equality in a multicultural society or in the context of conflict. Placing this model in the context of social politeness renders it irrelevant even to serious crimes, but White suggests that in the case of serious crimes or harms, the two sides need not live together, and hence the problem of forgiveness does not arise. This claim could be erroneous even in the context of interpersonal relations involving an offender and a victim—domestic violence comes to mind—and is similarly inaccurate in some cases of group conflict, as Marianna Papastephanou demonstrates:

> In most [communal conflict] cases, and especially where these involve dislocation, or the legitimation of dislocations, or demographic alterations and other crimes of war, a parting of the ways is impossible as well as morally unacceptable. It is also unacceptable because it may presuppose the false essentialist claim that some ethnic groups cannot live together peacefully. . . . In such contexts, the idea that a relaxed notion of forgiveness is useful to the relations of communities involved in longstanding conflicts has very limited relevance.[28]

In addition, this relaxed model of forgiveness as a social nicety is embedded in Western, English-speaking social norms and can hardly be translatable to other contexts and cultures.[29] It is hardly acceptable even from a religious Christian perspective,[30] and in cultures that view forgiveness as an abandonment of that part in one's past that was wronged, forgiveness can be understood as demeaning to the victim (or to wronged family members) and in no way as an offhanded nicety. Moreover, these models are stripped of historical context, rendering the educational efforts out of touch with the historical and social specificities of the communities in which they are practiced. If we teach that one must always work on one's internal ability to grant forgiveness, mainly in the hardest of circumstances when she suffered the worst harms, we place the burden of reconciliation solely or mainly on the victim, in addition to replicating the power relations that made her victim. In addition, such an educational approach may inadvertently teach lack of liability to potential offenders—they can sense that they are a priori forgiven without any demand for punishment or reparation.

All three models—the unconditional, the strict, and the relaxed—are focused on the victim; in other words, they put a lot of emphasis, following the Western religious traditions, on the moral requirement to forgive. The morality that they endorse is based on the perspective of the victim, her entitlements, and her duties. The educational approach that they endorse is focused on teaching students to consider their commitments and their possible responses to instances of harm done to them. A change

107

of perspective can be useful for the purposes of expansive education, as is suggested in the next section.

LEARNING TO BE FORGIVEN

For the purpose of teaching forgiveness in the context of intergroup and international conflict, two variations on the above-described models are required. First, the model should give attention not only to the perspective of the forgiving side but also to the side seeking forgiveness. Second, the model that would best serve the educational needs on the road toward peace is one that gives a proper place to claims of justice.

"Mea Culpa"

A public acknowledgment of past wrongs done by one's group to another, accompanied by an appropriate apology—an acceptance of moral responsibility—can open the door for peaceful relations among former rivals. Certain political actors manifested a similar sentiment by apologizing for historical wrongs done by the nations they represent to other nations and minority groups.[31]

The sentiment expressed in this type of public apology frames the model that is the most relevant one for expansive education. It is an alternative to the three models described above, in that it is focused not on the duty of the victim to forgive but on the responsibility of the offender to seek forgiveness. In this it parts from the Abrahamic traditions and turns our moral and educational attention to the offender. One author claims that it is dangerous "to focus so much on the duty to forgive," particularly in an educational setting, because of the risk of encouraging an egocentric perspective that "no matter what we do or how we deal with it" forgiveness would be granted.[32] Learning to demand forgiveness stands the risk of feeding unequal power relations rather than overcoming them. Overcoming anger and blame would more readily occur not through obliged forgiveness but rather through a sincere acknowledgment of wrongs and a common attempt to establish the grounds for peaceful relations. It is important to stress that in most conflicts, there is rarely one side that is victimized and another that is completely evil and one-sidedly perpetrates wrongdoing. In most cases both sides have grievances that would justifiably be described as worthy of considering and amending.[33] Striving to acknowledge wrongdoing and requesting forgiveness is a key component of reverse patriotism as an aspect of expansive education. By expanding members' awareness of historical perspectives that are not necessarily triumphalistic neither depict the group as a victim but rather point to the group's wrongdoing, a more morally complex view of both history and morality could be constructed without abandoning national sentiments.

The history curriculum is typically an educational site in which forms of recognition, acknowledgment, and forgiveness can be negotiated and expressed. Learning to regard ourselves and the group with which we identify as blameworthy from some other group's perspective can be a sobering educational exercise. More often than not, schools focus on "us" as a morally blameless entity. The pressures of subgroups who suffer past or present injustices are a possible force that may change the curriculum into a more inclusive and reflective one. The representation in the history curriculum in American schools of blacks and Native Americans and the complex history of injustice they suffered was made possible through the pressure of groups within the academic and sociopolitical arenas. Learning to acknowledge the complex relations among social groups can thus generate the first steps in the social process of forgiveness. The same can happen in the context of international conflict when groups learn to acknowledge the historical complexities through which their relations were formed. For this to happen, the education system needs to rise above what Theodor Adorno calls "national vanity" or "narcissistic nationalism"[34] and to consider the national group in which it operates as part of a complex relational international order in which no one is perfectly just.

Just Forgiveness

As for the second modification required in order to delineate a conception of forgiveness suitable for the purposes of expansive education, the role that justice plays in the facilitation of forgiveness has to be carefully crafted. A proper response to claims of

109

justice must not waive them, but it must also refrain from a strict economic formation of justice (such as "an eye for an eye") as a precondition for forgiveness. For the purpose of peace building and preserving democratic attitudes, relinquishing the demand for justice, as the relaxed or "no problem" model expects, cannot suffice. True, this may be an appropriate approach for groups already living in harmony in a liberal democracy. But when a group is striving to create peaceful relations, when it is actively involved in war but still aims to preserve democratic or liberal inclinations, it may need a more comprehensive form of education beyond teaching the "no problem" response.

A pertinent approach to forgiveness should take into account claims of historical and even personal injustice and respond to them in an environment receptive to forgiveness. This does not mean that all claims can indeed be answered to their fullest. But it does mean that they should be sincerely acknowledged. Forgiveness must presuppose justice, at least in a loose sense of the mutual acknowledgment of wrongs and the mutual understanding that these wrongs are not to be repeated. In reflecting on the guilt of one's own group, one learns to seek forgiveness "for the culpability that remains after excuses, justifications, restitution and repentant reforms have been made and accepted—a culpability that warrants our continuing to be resented."[35] Thus, as in the public education display of the South African Truth and Reconciliation Commission, it is more important to acknowledge past wrongs in an effort to bring about reconciliation than to pursue justice in its retaliatory form. Still, a challenge to the power relations that generated the conflict and injustice is a minimal condition for forgiveness that presupposes justice.

In the context of group conflict, this challenge to power relations is ideally expressed in the discussion of forgiveness that is based on publicly accessible declarations and expressions of seeking and granting forgiveness. Absent the access to emotional aspects of forgiveness that are fundamental to the interpersonal context, intergroup forgiveness has to be presented in public forms, education being a principal form among the nondeclaratory ones. The declarative spectrum of forgiveness includes politicians and leaders publicly asking or granting forgiveness for past wrongs (acknowledging them is the basis for this act). It also includes moments that can serve as public epiphanies, such as the celebratory signing of a peace treaty (in the case of international conflict) or a cordial meeting between leaders of adversary sides. Beyond such public declarations, teaching about the other side and learning to see history and current affairs from the other's perspective is a crucial, ongoing method of generating appropriate conditions for acknowledging the other's perspective, accepting blame, and enabling forgiveness. Hence, the inclusion of various perspectives of history in the public education system serves the purpose of overcoming the dehumanization of the other side. In addition, it serves the purpose of inducing forgiveness by publicly acknowledging the harm one's side caused the other and the justifiability of the other's claims. This is by no means a simple demand, as the debate on patriotic education exemplifies.[36] In wartime there is a growing demand to teach a narrow form of patriotic history and to incorporate triumphalist patriotism into the curriculum. But it is crucial to maintain compatible (rather than adversary) forms of communal memories, and to incorporate them into a humane conception at the other. This would serve both the preservation of democratic attitudes and for the establishment of a basis for a common peaceful future. Thus, reversing and expanding the teaching of patriotic histories and revising and expanding collective memory are fundamental aspects of seeking forgiveness.

How do we reconcile the remembrance of past wrongs and the possibility of forgiveness? Avishai Margalit claims that one has an obligation to oneself to overcome painful memories in order to restore her own well-being. He states that "successful forgiveness is not forgetting the wrong done but rather overcoming the resentment that accompanies it."[37] For Margalit, and in a way for Minow too, the claim is not from the agent who seeks forgiveness but rather from the victim herself.[38] Considering both the well-being of the offender and that of the victim brings forth the fact that it is clearly in the interest of both to reach a state of forgiveness. In the interpersonal context this state is hard to achieve for various psychological reasons, including an urge to revenge, a perception of the harm as irreversible, and a lack of trust, which leads to a disbelief in the wrongdoer's apology or repentance.[39] All these aspects exist in the intergroup context as well, but they are more accessible, at least in their public manifestations. Apologies, restitutions, and the

Expansive Education

DEMOCRATIC SOCIETIES struggling to live through a protracted conflict while preserving their social formation and political structure face many challenges. The expansive education response to these challenges is based on balancing the demands of belligerent citizenship with democratic principles and a realistic vision of peace. In the realm of political ethics, this challenge coincides with the attempt to maintain civil liberties without compromising security. This undertaking offers the proper ethical background for the educational project advocated in this book, which is focused on the tendency of the public education system to reflect and replicate the social responses to war, termed here "belligerent citizenship." It is important to realize that there is no easy way to resolve the problem of democracy under threat, that both extreme political ways are unsatisfactory: "[A]n ethics of balance cannot privilege rights above all ... or public safety above all. This is the move—privileging one to the exclusion of the other—that produces moral error."[1] Expressing suspicion for each act, law, or practice meant to enhance security is impracticable and unjustified; rejecting civil liberties as soft-hearted luxuries creates the risk of losing the free society, or in Michael Ignatieff's words, not recognizing ourselves in the mirror.

This effort to balance conflicting demands is uniquely challenging during a protracted conflict. Such conflicts have vague aims, and thus their ends are hard to define (it might never be appropriate to claim, "Mission accomplished"). Even the declaration of war is often not a clear act but an evolving series of acts and responses. Therefore, Just War theory in its commonly accepted form[2] is insufficient for responding to all aspects of protracted and broadly defined conflicts such as the "war on terror." To address the increasingly demanding challenges that many countries around the world face today, Just War theory needs to be expanded. The assumption in the background of this book is that social dimensions need to be added to the moral-political arguments of Just War—dimensions that will support the preservation of democracy in a democratic society involved in such conflict. Expansive education is an attempt at outlining one such dimension.

Expansive education is designed to incorporate the social perspectives instigated by security threats into a democratic notion of civic education. In other words, it is meant to accommodate some of the most pressing social needs, expectations, and tendencies in times of war, those that are justifiably characterized as supporting the aim of endurance, stability, and survival into a democratic theory of education. Many authors agree that a main justification of publicly funded education is the ability of such a system to cultivate attitudes and skills that are considered to be prerequisites of a stable democratic polity.[3] Since the circumstances of a national conflict, along with their social consequences, imperil democracy in many ways, it is public educators' role to encourage democracy in the face of these threats. Democratic education, modified by the relevant aspects derived from feminist, multicultural, and peace education approaches, emerges as a subversive act. It goes against the mainstream of belligerent citizenship, but without losing sight of its inevitable aspects that provide what is necessary for social endurance nor compromising the principles upon which a democratic society is founded. The subversive mission of opposing rather than accommodating public expectations is evident in expansive education's insistence on supporting diverse (rather than narrowed-down) constructions of public agenda, acceptable opinions, and forms of patriotism. However, this insistence is mitigated by the responsive accommodation of (certain versions of) the beliefs and attitudes necessary for socially surviving conflict. In particular, the need for a communal belief in social unity can be endorsed by the public education system without the intolerance and exclusion it sometimes entails, through fostering a conceptualization of citizenship as shared fate, as well as reverse forms of patriotism. The framework of democratic education, when informed by the conceptualization of citizenship and national membership as shared fate, is thus amended to include recognition, peace building, forgiveness, and the shared effort to create a diverse public agenda and a positive vision of the future. All these are to be strived for through the mechanisms of civic education.

114

The role of the public education system in the realm of civic education is twofold. First, it needs to assess the contents and the definitions of good citizenship as those apply to society at large as well as to the school system. Second, it needs to develop mechanisms by which this good citizenship will be promoted. Part of the first role, the assessment of good citizenship, calls for an evaluation of existing social perceptions on the topic; however, the commitment of a justifiable public education system is not just to take into account the current preferences of the community or society in which it operates and which it serves. It must also account for the good of that community or society as manifested in a long-term appraisal of its structure and spirit. At heart, the public education system is an institution that needs to continuously balance the present with the future—to respond, in its vision and the sum of its actions, both to the demands of the sociopolitical context in which it functions and to the broader, forward-looking commitments to the basic values of society's political traditions and visions.

Civic education in democratic societies converges significantly with education for democracy. In democratic countries an essential aspect of being a citizen involves knowledge (formal and practical) of the institutions and processes through which democracy is realized, as well as the attitudes and skills to express this knowledge. The desirable convergence between the fundamental demands of civic and democratic education becomes more relevant in times of war—times that may generate a significant challenge to citizens' democratic commitments.

American thought on democratic education is historically divided into two trends. The first is a more conservative trend, associated with classical liberalism and contemporary libertarianism, which focuses on education for democracy mainly in the context of liberties, training toward productive participation in the market economy, and other individualistic values.[4] The second trend is the public conceptualization of education for democracy, which entails an enhanced focus on social and civic aspects of democratic values and practices. Although I find the two trends not to be as starkly at odds as they are sometimes portrayed,[5] the ideas presented here are more closely linked to the conception of education for public democracy. However, both the liberal and the radical conceptualizations of education

115

for public democracy fall short in the realm discussed here—namely, the proper educational responses to the challenges that a society in conflict faces. For example, David Sehr's notion of public democracy as an educational ideal is constructed against a presumed background of civic disengagement, which is less easily presumed in times of conflict, as seen in the American example of the responses to the 9/11 attacks and youth political mobilization during the 2004 election.[6] In addition, most debates on education for public democracy are based on assumed ideological pluralism, which is also not to be taken for granted in times of war and protracted conflicts. In circumstances of a narrowed public debate and suppressed diversity, civic education for democracy needs to be modified.

Consider one widely quoted representation of education for democracy in the post–9/11 world:

> Our children are living in perilous times. To prepare them to preserve their heritage of freedom in this dangerous world, we must place education aimed at cultivating democratic citizenship at the heart of the school curriculum.[7]

This description of the educational consequences of security threats relies on a premise that many share: the need to "cultivate democratic citizenship" is one of the premises of expansive education as well. However, the two central components of this education, as suggested by the quote that follows, are more questionable: "First, our young people should come to understand—and embrace—the principles of liberty, equality, and justice. . . . They should learn about the institutions . . . and . . . historical roots." This much is broadly agreed upon. The second component is more controversial, in particular the list of qualities that the author describes as the "mark of true citizens: courage, loyalty, responsibility, gratitude to forebears, and a self-sacrificing devotion to the common good . . . they must have . . . a love for—and desire to perpetuate—the republic."[8]

These qualities are the marks of citizenship only inasmuch as citizenship is perceived in its belligerent form as a communal identity and nationalism as a project of loyalty and sacrifice, rather than supplementing this perception with the notions of shared fate and reverse patriotism.[9] Kersten, for example, advocates the teaching of "character ideal" through heroic stories of patriotism; she emphasizes the need to inspire students to follow suit in the footsteps of national heroes.[10] The conceptions of civic virtue and patriotism that serve as its basis of civic education are detrimentally narrow. They are derived from a perception of citizenship solely as identity and of national character as only marginally open for deliberation and adaptation. Those notions of patriotism and nationality, although compatible with democracy in many ways, are nonetheless undesirable for a nation that fosters pluralism and inclusion as essential components of its institutions and spirit.

When the discussion is set against the background of public schools' tendency to shy away from political education, there is ample reason to think about how the civic curriculum needs to be revised even before introducing conflict and its effects. The circumstances of conflict, and in particular belligerent citizenship, make it vital to accommodate further notions such as gender equality, acknowledgment, and forgiveness into a strong democratic education curriculum. Such a curriculum would be committed to promoting the values, attitudes, and behaviors necessary for the preservation of democracy while remaining responsive to the social demands of conflict. In other words, it is essential to combine curricula and pedagogies such as the ones described in the previous chapters from peace education, feminist, and multicultural approaches with a strong democratic education. Many of the tools developed in these theoretical approaches and practical enterprises can be used for the purpose of responding constructively to the needs of a democratic society at war. The inclusion of peace and democracy in public schools' civic education curriculum can respond to the social needs of a society for endurance while preserving the democratic formal and moral structure that gives meaning both to the institutions of public education and to the endurance of society. It provides a comprehensive response to belligerent citizenship, endorsing some of its aspects while amending others. It does so out of a strong belief in the power of education to transform society while preserving its basic tenets.

117

"More than a half century of empirical research . . . points to the consistent and overwhelming influence of education on myriad facets of democratic citizenship."[11] Most of the empirical research on education maintains the approach that "the more, the better"—namely, the more education attainment, the more civic engagement and political participation can be traced, both individually and statistically. These findings are supported with a further conclusion—not just any educational attainment would do; specifically, an education that involves a social civic curriculum, an education that emphasizes verbal skills and supports public mindedness, increases the likelihood of a student's participation in the many aspects of political life.[12] Many studies point to the fact that more civic education means better civic outcomes when those outcomes are measured in civic knowledge, skills, and behavior.[13]

Civic participation and engagement are imperative for the legitimacy of democracy; creating citizens who are civic minded is thus a vital role of public education. When democratic stability is threatened by external perils such as terror attacks and conflict and by correlating internal responses such as the suspension of rights and a narrowing public agenda, civic education becomes an even more crucial factor for the preservation of a stable democracy. In wartime, societies experience a surge in political interest as manifested in news consumption,[14] political knowledge, and the willingness to participate in protests or rallies, spurred by a sense of renewed patriotism and commitment to the public good. This public interest in the political sphere, however, does not always work to strengthen democratic commitments, particularly when participation takes the form of belligerent citizenship, which reinforces national identification rather than demonstrating broader democratic interests that can be informed by a sense of shared fate. Hence, the increase in civic participation may be considered good news to those who, following Putnam, are concerned with the decline in civic engagement. However, the forms of participation—and the types of commitments that this participation seems to express and reinforce—leave much to be desired, particularly in times when patriotism does not always coincide with a commitment to democracy.

Most approaches presented in the preceding chapters contribute to the effort of creating citizens in times of war in one particular area, namely, that of learning to overcome a history of adversarial relations and live peacefully. Peace education scholarship provides some helpful, practical tools for the formation of productive encounters with adversarial groups; feminist pedagogy develops invaluable instruments for teaching nonviolence and recognition within existing educational institutions and frameworks while resisting their undesirable effects. Multicultural politics and education encourage acknowledgment and forgiveness and at their best can offer both insights into overcoming animosity and tools for a successful educational implementation of these insights.

These various contributions focus on learning to maintain social cooperation through awareness of other perspectives. This is helpful both during conflict and when peace arrives. How can they fit in with the reinforcement of democratic values, attitudes and behaviors in the face of belligerent civic tendencies?

The challenges facing democratic scholars and educators in wartime are multifaceted, and the response offered here is meant to be correspondingly complex. The challenges include the need to differentiate aspects of belligerent citizenship that are supportive of social endurance from those that threaten democratic values or commitments. As I suggested, social unity and patriotism, when interpreted as part of a conceptual framework of social membership as shared fate, can be considered acceptable aspects of belligerent citizenship for the purposes of expansive education. Enduring war while preserving democracy requires a conscious effort to oppose the emergence of a culture of war, which is inimical both to democracy and to maintaining a vision of peace. The culture of war is expressed in the domination of the security discourse over most public debates, the narrowing of the public agenda, and the priority given to security concerns over most other policy considerations. To realize their mandate as the public servants most essentially responsible for the preservation of democracy, public educators need to accommodate recognition of the "other," acknowledgment of wrongs, seeking and giving forgiveness, and the broadest public debate possible into a framework of democratic education. Thus, they can adapt the conception of democratic education to meet the social challenges and requirements of a society at war.

Expansive education at its best is structured as an educational manifestation of citizenship as shared fate, by focusing on the curricular and pedagogical expressions of social and national membership as participation in a joint project. Students and communities are invited to take part in the mutual formation of visions of society's values and its future, thus contributing to social strength and unity—broadly construed—while supporting democratic attitudes and skills. Endorsing, as I did, a description of nationality as a shared fate rather than solely as an aspect of identity is both a descriptive and a public educational project. Citizenship is a normative aspect of personal and public life inasmuch as it reflects not a given feature of the social fabric or personal character, but rather an ongoing task of reconciling collective commitments with democratic principles.

Perceiving identity as the sole basis of national affiliation could turn nationalism into a divisive endeavor, for it generates an expectation for a potentially exclusive unified basis. Although nationalism thus perceived could endorse pluralism, it does not necessitate an acceptance of pluralism, and thus it could be hard to use as a tool against repressive forms of patriotism in times of conflict. Even in other times, perceiving nationalism as a form of identity can potentially be demeaning in its requirement to abandon a host of aspects of individual or group-related particularities when those do not coincide with (or are hostile to) the national identity.

Conversely, learning to conceive of citizenship as shared fate can cultivate a more open and inclusive form of national affiliation. In a way that may initially seem contradictory, the pluralistic and open-ended nature of this form of nationalism can in fact be more unifying than the more rigid conception of nationalism as identity. The host of institutions, laws, histories, natural resources, economy, and elected representatives, as well as identities that make up our shared fate, are all open to a variety of interpretations, deliberation, and influence on the part of individuals and groups within the nation. The aspects of the actual and conceptual network that holds a society together are open to change and evolvement. This open-ended shared project is a manifestation of reverse patriotism, which aims to incorporate multiple expressions of the love of country. Public schools committed to expansive education can develop students' commitments to the notion of shared fate that includes both an understanding of the basic affiliation we have with one another and the provisional nature of most aspects of the actual affiliation within the limits of democratic principles. Thus, expansive education can maintain plurality of opinion as well as tolerance while still cultivating the attitudes relevant for enduring conflict.

The concept of expansive education shares with the notion of citizenship as shared fate the open-mindedness that is the benchmark of inclusion and pluralism; yet both are not limitless in their acceptance of a wide range of perspectives. Both notions are bounded by the understanding of the basic democratic principles of equality and liberty and the way they should interplay in the making of democratic institutions. Both endorse pluralism as a required social manifestation of democracy—citizenship as shared fate is based on a concept of legitimacy that arises from mutual justification, which in turn is the result of civic equality and reciprocal respect. Expansive education is fundamentally aimed at cultivating a commitment to civic engagement in the process of such mutual justification and at endorsing a host of views that maintain both democratic and national commitments. Understanding and experiencing the importance of exposure to a plural environment of perspectives, affiliations, and interpretations are necessary steps toward engaging in the mutual process of justification that legitimizes a democratic community of shared fate.

These features make the conceptions of citizenship and education discussed here not only compatible but also suitable to together, offer a potentially fruitful response to the social burdens of conflict and their ensuing needs. Expansive education is thus one pragmatic manifestation of citizenship as shared fate; it is a translation of the expectations and contributions of this conception of citizenship into the realm of education, particularly in a state of threat.

Seyla Benhabib suggests that engaging in a democratic discourse in a diverse society requires a capacity for what Immanuel Kant calls "enlarged thought."[15] Melissa Williams takes up this contention in her discussion of citizenship as shared fate by

121

asserting the requirement for democratic citizenship under conditions of "sometimes-unwelcome diversity."[16] She describes three basic features of citizenship education in multicultural democracies, which constitute the conditions for enlarged thought: diversity, recognition of the "other," and learning through exercise. In what follows, I describe expansive education as an application of this theoretical approach to civic education in wartime. I interpret these three features as corresponding with the demands of preserving democracy in times of conflict, but as still requiring some adaptations to make them suitable for addressing the consequences of belligerent citizenship. First, teaching diversity in times of confining social unity should take into account the complexities of working in an environment that may not be susceptible to diversity of opinion and perspective. In addition, expanding on the notion of "exercise," I suggest that civic education in wartime in particular must be exercised and expressed as a political endeavor. Differing from most common approaches to peace education and from many conflict resolution and multicultural education projects that focus on interpersonal relations, expansive education must be portrayed as a political, sometimes subversive attempt to support democracy and peace as expressed in the political realm. This political aspect of civic education is an essential part of expansive education. How does the amended notion of enlarged thought figure into the political task of expansive education?

The first task of expansive education, then, is to create and support diversity rather than respond to descriptive circumstances of a multiplicity of opinions. To achieve diversity in times of war, the public education system needs to become inclusive in terms of perspectives, issues, and persons. This can be practiced through a conscious expansion of the scope of topics discussed and standpoints tolerated. The cultivation of a wide variety of perspectives needs to be an active engagement on the part of teachers and students, to avoid the spiraling silence of "other" points of view.[17] When continuously performed in schools, it can feed the public's commitment to diversity as well as its tolerance.

Consider the aims of democratic education as portrayed in Amy Gutmann's influential theory. The primary aim of public education in a democracy, according to Gutmann, is to educate children for free and equal citizenship. This aim is to be realized through deliberation on the contents of public education, limited by democratic values.[18] As Gutmann maintains, "Schooling that is publicly mandated . . . may legitimately pursue civic purposes, which include . . . tolerance and mutual respect."[19] In the context of belligerent citizenship, the public education system must begin by addressing the question of its accountability to social demands and expectations, including the question of parental authority. What if belligerent citizenship, including narrowly conceived patriotic unity, is what most parents want for their children? Democratic education reminds us that the expectation of parents and communities cannot replace the public education system's commitment to basic democratic principles.[20] It is clear that a democratic education is not dependent entirely on social consensus. Rather it is derived from democratic principles and commitments, which provide the basis and the moral limits for educational practices. Gutmann describes democratic education as opposing blind patriotism and converging with a love of country inasmuch as this love manifests a commitment to defend democratic ideals. Patriotism as an educational aim cannot evade these basic moral boundaries and should offer ways of interpreting and manifesting them.[21] When democracy is widely endorsed in society, the teaching of patriotism can be achieved in compliance with democratic principles. In wartime, when uncritical patriotic education stands the risk of promoting parochialism and injustice, expansive education must express its commitment to democracy by endorsing reverse patriotism and a wider understanding of nationhood. When parents oppose teaching their children a democratic, civic curricula (as in *Mozert*[22]), they "do not have a general right to override otherwise legitimate democratic decisions concerning the schooling of their children."[23] It is therefore the school's commitment to democracy that takes precedence over any demand made by specific parents or groups regarding the civic education of children. This claim, widely accepted by political, educational, and legal commentators in the context of *Mozert*, should be extended to include situations in which the social majority rejects the educational commitment to substantive democracy. The democratic argument for committing the public education system to the principles of democracy, not to majority rule or parental authority, should be maintained in better and worse times. In better times it may entail enforcing specific curricula on dissenting parents or enforcing diversity against social tendencies of segregation. In times of war, the public education system should continue to exercise its commitment to democracy through opposing the undemocratic messages of belligerent citizenship. Thus, the aims of democratic education must be preserved as part of the principles that inform expansive education, but their interpretation and the pedagogic and curricular tools that are used to implement them need to be adapted to correspond to the needs of society at war. It may be politically unwise for school boards to declare a commitment to social change or enlarged thought. However, it would be possible and desirable to define the cultivation of democratic values as an educational goal. In the social circumstances of wartime, when the public may be inclined toward a narrower, less inclusive form of patriotism within and outside the schools, democratic education in its expansive form may need to impose exposure to diversity rather than striving to accommodate it. It may need to focus on the cultivation of other basic democratic values, not only in small, radical groups but in a growing part of mainstream society as well. The sound justifications democratic education offers for imposing basic democratic principles on marginal groups in a democratic society apply also to circumstances in which these values are questioned or rejected by large parts of the mainstream.

Thus, before diversity can be acknowledged or celebrated as democratic education expects, it must descriptively be present in the classroom. Part of what enables the perpetuation of belligerent citizenship is the reduction of the public agenda to questions of security, which are expected to be solved by military and administrative professionals. Here too the role of teachers—as educators and as public intellectuals—is to resist the attenuation of the public sphere and the public agenda by creating a zone of vivid democratic life within the classroom. Expansive education requires educators to oppose the social tendency to narrow the borders of the public agenda. The discussion of issues other than those relevant to security is emancipatory, for it reclaims politics as a sphere of political judgments and value choices. It makes room for a multiplicity of perspectives on a variety of questions and gives voice to those whose perspectives and interests are being silenced by the overpowering claims of national security.

In such times there is a great urgency to inculcate the values necessary for the perpetuation of democratic institutions. This can occur either (preferably) in the representation of various groups and perspectives by the students' and teachers' bodies or through a proper representation of differences. As pluralism and diversity are fundamental in the moral domain and central to the preservation of just democracy, it is the role of democratic public schools to maintain such diversity in the public sphere of their institutions.[24]

Hence, when dealing with questions such as how to practice patriotic education, expansive education responds by construing patriotism as a derivation of citizenship as shared fate. In other words, patriotic education needs to be informed by a notion of social and national membership not as individual and group identity, but rather as arising from linked fate. Individuals sharing some aspects of their lives, such as territory, language, traditions, and perceived history, can learn as part of their civic and democratic education to relate to this shared fate as the constitutive aspect of their national affiliation and identity. Through an open discussion on the possibilities of jointly structuring a shared public agenda, and an inclusive debate on the consequences of this agenda for people of various ethnicities, religions, genders, and ideological stances, nationality can be expressed as shared fate. In addition, shared fate as part of "reciprocity beyond borders"[25] can support the generation of a culture of peace by expressing the aspects of linked fate between the nation and its neighbors (and the globe). This is a form of responding positively to the moral reality of nationalism, namely, the existing communal affiliation of individuals and their sense of belonging, as well as to the rigidity of these sentiments when the nation is perceived as facing threats. The expansive education response is constructed around the espousal of these sentiments while providing a proper framework of perceiving them as shared fate in order to accommodate them within the framework of democratic education.

Expansive education, like enlarged thought, relies on the substantial usage of classroom diversity through curricular and other activities. This use is made to support the ability of students to put themselves in the position of the "other" and to

125

share the other's experiences. Some of the most productive curricular and pedagogic tools of endorsing and encouraging diversity are adapted from feminist and multicultural literature. These perspectives are useful for expansive education because they are focused on expanding the knowledge of students (and teachers) beyond their immediate experiences, and beyond formal academic knowledge, in order to know people and cultures different from themselves. Employing diversity in positive ways can help celebrate it in the ethnic and cultural sense and support democracy in a society that does not always welcome all forms of diversity. This usage of diversity to develop students' minds and hearts in democratically oriented ways is one of the essential aspects of expansive education. It embodies the endorsement of descriptive (ethnic, cultural, religious) diversity while encouraging the development of diversity in ideological stances and in conceptions of the political. The positive employment of diversity in this dual sense is tied to learning to acknowledge both differences and similarities among people of various backgrounds and viewpoints. A complementing form of learning to acknowledge the other is through generating dialogue among rival groups, whether through actual meetings or through learning about them, and creating a shared and equal dialogue among them. As Henry Giroux reminds us, the role of educators is to "provide spaces of resistance within the public schools . . . while simultaneously providing the knowledge and skills that enlarge their sense of the social and their possibilities as viable agents capable of expanding and deepening democratic public life."[26] Actively supporting the expression of a variety of standpoints rather than plainly responding to their implied existence in the public and educational arenas would be an effective practice of manifesting students' civic equality. It would demonstrate a resistance to the exclusion of individuals and groups by the security-dominated, solidarity-oriented public sphere.

Acknowledgment, as a form of overcoming dehumanization and creating bridges beyond (former) adversaries, can complement the generation of diversity by expressing the complexities of social and historical processes. Learning to acknowledge and analyze the moral complexities of a conflict is a necessary step toward being able to seek forgiveness and grant it. Hence, the notions of diversity, acknowledgment and forgiveness, as these terms are used here, are all tied together as part of the broader concept of expansive education. Studying moral and historical complexities and learning to consider complex views on patriotism can encourage an acceptance of one's group as carrying moral responsibility in the historical processes that made it what it is today. It can mean accepting the notion of one's group as one that may need to seek forgiveness on certain past events and grant forgiveness on others. The conception of national membership as shared fate can educationally contribute to the process by teaching citizens to view the interpretation of the past as part of their moral commitment to the community and as a basis for designing a mutually acceptable vision of the future, rather than viewing such interpretation as an assault on an aspect of one's own identity.

All of these notions, as the guiding principles of expansive education, should be available for interpretation in specific contexts of ongoing and diminishing conflicts. Although they can be employed in various ways, their expression in the different contexts should maintain two interrelated main features. First, their implementation is to be realized through exercise. The personal experience of conflict factors into the conceptualization of conflict, peace, and related issues in the minds of young people. If an educational program is to respond to this conceptualization in productive ways and help shape a positive vision of the future in people who witnessed or experienced the violence of war, the educational approach cannot rely on cognition alone. Pedagogy and curricula that seek to have an impact on perception and behavior must combine cognitive (or academic) aspects with emotional and social components. They must be based on the recognition that all these aspects—the psychological, the cognitive, and the social—interplay in the formation of perceptions and attitudes related to conflict as well as to democracy.

Second, beyond recognition and its employment in the formation of curricular materials and pedagogic approaches, the contextual interpretation of expansive education must always be based on an understanding of education as a political endeavor. Learning through exercise and contextualizing the study of democracy and civics requires not only pedagogic responses to students' lived experiences but also a commitment to a politicized approach.

We are not born with an enlarged thought, nor can we learn it solely in a theoretical fashion. Only through the repeated exercise of the emotional and cognitive capacities as offered through expansive education can we acquire the ability to widen the horizons of our social perceptions. The exercise of enlarged thought depends on politicized encounters with diversity; the emergence of enlarged thought depends upon a discursive exchange between different perspectives. Encouraging the emergence of enlarged thought relies on the diversification of the participants in the educational process. In this the practice of expansive education as a political endeavor ties together the demands of diversity, acknowledgment, and recognition—it situates diversity as a welcomed factor in classroom interaction, it encourages its development or sustaining, and it supports the positive exchange among a multiplicity of backgrounds, opinions, and perspectives as a pedagogic and educational tool.

Further details of expansive education cannot be spelled out beyond the context of a specific community conflict. Educators and policy makers committed to expansive education should aim to overcome specific challenges, to acknowledge a specific "other," to strengthen identifiable democratic commitments in the face of particular threats. Responding to the lived experiences of students is an immanent part of any proper civic education.[27] In wartime, when the perception of war, peace, and related concepts in the minds of children are gravely affected by their experiences, the localization, concretization, and politicization of civic studies become more urgent than ever. Through these educational processes and their possible reverberation in the public sphere, conflicting groups can learn to envision actual futures of peace, including the challenges they generate and possible ways for overcoming them, together or apart. One of the gravest threats facing public education in times of war is a lack of vision for the future. Politics devoid of positive visions of the future can degenerate into stagnant conceptions of society and where it is (and should be) heading. Therefore, democracy has to be struggled for, and this struggle should become the central role of the public education system in times of war. To envision a different future, different questions must be asked, and differing answers should be tolerated to the largest extent possible. Envisioning a future of peace entails questioning the basic assumptions of war as well as the social acceptance of these assumptions. It entails the development of critical thought that is limited only by the broadest and most basic democratic political values, rather than by the contingencies of public opinion.

The educational process is central to the generation of communal, including national, affiliations. It is the site where citizens learn to examine and consider their common grounds. At its best it can be a site where different views of history are presented and debated and different visions of the common future are explored. Through this process, children can establish a sense of themselves as future citizens and develop a perception of their social and national group. Expansive education is meant to accommodate critical appraisals of social perceptions and convictions; it is structured to enable the expression of many forms of patriotism, including reverse patriotism. It aims to support the deliberative reinterpretation of the practices, traditions, and visions that inform our shared fate, without accepting any of them as given and without losing sight of the vitality of maintaining (rather than deconstructing) a diverse but still shared vision of this fate. The democratic, peace-building goal of expansive education is expressed by expanding the moral understanding of citizenship, cultivating multiple ways of being a good citizen, and encouraging an acceptance of this multiplicity in the minds of the next generation of fellow citizens.

Notes

Introduction

1. Susan Sontag, *Regarding the Pain of Others* (New York: Farrar, Straus & Giroux, 2003), 74.

Chapter 1
Citizenship in Wartime

1. A compilation of views on citizenship, mostly in contemporary times, is presented in Gershon Shafir, ed., *The Citizenship Debates: A Reader* (Minneapolis: University of Minnesota Press, 1998). A multidimensional description of citizenship in its relations to civic education is offered in Orit Ichilov, *Citizenship and Citizenship Education in a Changing World* (London: Woburn Press, 1998), 11–27. A comprehensive historical perspective on American citizenship can be found in Rogers Smith, *Civic Ideals: Conflicting Visions of Citizenship in U.S. History* (New Haven, CT: Yale University Press, 1997).

2. See, for example, the critical description by Seyla Benhabib, *Situating the Self* (Cambridge, UK: Polity Press, 1992), chap. 3.

3. T. H. Marshall, *Class, Citizenship, and Social Development* (New York: Anchor Books, 1965), in particular the essay "Citizenship and Social Class."

4. Liah Greenfeld, *Nationalism: Five Roads to Modernity* (Cambridge, MA: Harvard University Press, 1993).

5. Iris Marion Young, "Feminist Reactions to the Contemporary Security Regime," *Hypatia* 18:1 (2003): 223–31.

6. Main interpretations of Hobbes's *Leviathan* suggest that he allowed for a vibrant civil society to exist within the limits of his Leviathan. I am referring here only to his basic justification for the establishment of the state.

7. Abraham Maslow, *Motivation and Personality*, 2nd ed. (New York: Harper & Row, 1970).

8. See Russell Hardin, "Civil Liberties in an Era of Mass Terrorism," *Journal of Ethics* 8:1 (2004): 77–95.

9. I chose to focus on democratic citizenship rather than on liberal democracy because the most pressing threats of belligerent citizenship are directed toward the principles of democracy and not necessarily those of liberalism.

10. For a description of some of these characteristics as they materialize in the Israeli public sphere, see Gad Barzilai, *Democracy in Time of War: Conflict and Consensus in Israel* (Tel Aviv: Sifriat Poalim, 1992) (in Hebrew); Baruch Kimmerling, *The Interrupted System: Israeli Civilians in War and Routine Times* (New Brunswick, NJ: Transaction Books, 1993).

11. For a variety of examples to this claim, see Yael Tamir, "Pro Patria Mori: Death and the State," in *The Morality of Nationalism*, ed. R. McKim and J. McMahan (Oxford: Oxford University Press, 1997). For the historical American context, see Cecilia Elizabeth O'Leary, *To Die For: The Paradox of American Patriotism* (Princeton, NJ: Princeton University Press, 1999).

12. For the Israeli context, see, e.g., Yitzhak Galnur, *The Beginning of Israeli Democracy* (Tel Aviv: Am Oved, 1985), 309ff. (in Hebrew); Orit Ichilov, "Patterns of Functioning of a Citizen in a Democracy," in *Education for Citizenship in a Democracy*, ed. Orit Ichilov (Tel Aviv: Masada and Tel Aviv University, 1993) (in Hebrew). This change in the construction of civic participation is less significant to the theory of civic education, mainly because education is a nonvoluntary system, and therefore it will mostly remain in the background for the rest of the discussion. The current war on terrorism, however, began with a plea from the president to go shopping. Civic participation in the war effort was deemed marginal, and the surge in feelings of patriotism and volunteerism in the American public sphere was relegated to contributions to the Red Cross and the planning of local memorial sites. This failure to build on the civic responses to 9/11 was criticized by many political commentators and researchers. See symposium on civic engagement in the post–9/11 world (the word "world" here refers to the United States) in *PS: Political Science and Politics* 35:3 (September 2002). For example, in this symposium, Theda Skocpol expresses disappointment over the failure of the administration to revitalize American civic democracy after 9/11.

13. Daniel Bar-Tal, *The Rocky Road toward Peace* (Jerusalem: Hebrew University Press, 1996), 24 (in Hebrew).

14. CBS News, "Text of Zell Miller's RNC Speech," September 1, 2004, http://www.cbsnews.com/stories/2004/09/01/politics/main640299.shtml.

15. For an extensive empirical discussion of the political and civic consequences of the prolonged conflict on the Israeli political system, see Giora Goldberg, Gad Barzilai, and Efraim Inbar, *The Impact of Intercommunal Conflict: The Intifada and Israeli Public Opinion* (Jerusalem: Leonard Davis Institute, 1991); Gad Barzilai, *Wars, Internal Conflicts, and Political Order: A Jewish Democracy in the Middle East* (Albany: State University of New York Press, 1996).

16. For a discussion from both a contemporary and a historical perspective on the effects of conflict on free speech, see Jonathan R. Cole, "The Patriot Act on Campus," *Boston Review* (Summer 2003): 7–10.

17. For a thorough sociological discussion of historic and contemporary Israeli citizenship, see Gershon Shafir and Yoav Peled, *Being Israeli: The Dynamics of Multiple Citizenship* (Cambridge: Cambridge University Press, 2002). The authors tend to conclude that the pull toward liberalization and privatization is stronger in Israel these days; I suggest that this may be the case in certain periods but that overall, the dominance of security issues looms even in more quiet

times and readily tips the balance in the direction of a narrower, nationalist, or belligerent conception of citizenship.

18. Andrew J. Bacevich, *The New American Militarism: How Americans Are Seduced by War* (Oxford: Oxford University Press, 2005).

19. John E. Mueller, "Presidential Popularity from Truman to Johnson," *American Political Science Review* 64 (1970): 18–33; and *War, Presidents, and Public Opinion* (New York: Wiley, 1973).

20. Richard A. Brody, *Assessing the President* (Palo Alto, CA: Stanford University Press, 1991). Other researchers claim that there are other explanatory factors to the "rally effect," such as type of media coverage. See William D. Baker and John R. O'Neal, "Patriotism or Opinion Leadership?" *Journal of Conflict Resolution* 45:5 (October 2001): 661–87.

21. Rogers Smith, "The Mission to Promote Liberty Around the World" (presentation), American Political Science Association conference, Chicago, IL, September 2–5, 2004.

22. Michael Traugott and others, "How Americans Responded: A Study of Public Reactions to 9/11/01," *PS: Political Science and Politics* 35:3 (2002): 511–16, at 516.

23. A Gallup poll indicated 90 percent approval on September 21–22.

24. See preliminary findings in Brian J. Gaines, "Where's the Rally?" *PS: Political Science and Politics* 35:3 (September 2002): 531–36. See also R. K. Bird and E. B. Brandt, "Academic Freedom and 9/11: How the War on Terrorism Threatens Free Speech on Campus," *Communication Law and Policy* 7:4 (October 2002): 431–59. For an account of how the security discourse in America undermines basic civil liberties, see Bruce Shapiro, "All in the Name of Security," *Nation*, October 21, 2001, 20–21.

25. See Theda Skocpol, "Will 9/11 and the War on Terror Revitalize American Civic Democracy?" *PS: Political Science and Politics* 35:3 (September 2002): 537–40; Stanley B. Greenberg, " 'We'—Not 'Me': Public Opinion and the Return of the Government," *American Prospect* 12:22 (December 2001): 25–27.

26. See M. J. Dubnick, "Postscripts for a 'State of War': Public Administration and Civil Liberties after September 11," *Public Administration Review* 62 (September 2002): 86–91.

27. Dean Murphy, "Old Words on War Stirring a New Dispute," *New York Times*, January 14, 2003, A1. The decision was later reversed.

28. Quoted from a report by cnn.com, February 28, 2003.

29. Richard M. Fried, *The Russians Are Coming! The Russians Are Coming! Pageantry and Patriotism in Cold War America* (New York: Oxford University Press, 2003). A more popular book offering a variety of examples to the same effect is Richard J. Perry, *United We Stand: A Visual Journey of Wartime Patriotism* (Portland, OR: Collectors Press, 2002).

30. Sonya O. Rose, *Which People's War? National Identity and Citizenship in Wartime Britain, 1939–1945* (Oxford: Oxford University Press, 2003). This book

also offers evidence to the gendered notion of citizenship in wartime, which is discussed in more detail in chapter 4.

31. Kathryn M. Bindon, *More Than Patriotism: Canada at War, 1914–1918* (Toronto: Personal Library Publishers, 1979).

32. Carlton J. H. Hayes, *France, A Nation of Patriots* (New York: Columbia University Press, 1930).

33. Andrew Arato, "*Minima Politica* after September 11," *Constellations* 9:1 (2002): 46–52, at 47.

34. Iris Marion Young, *Justice and the Politics of Difference* (Princeton, NJ: Princeton University Press, 1990), 22.

35. Ibid.

36. Amy Gutmann and Dennis Thompson, *Why Deliberative Democracy?* (Princeton, NJ: Princeton University Press, 2004), chap. 1.

37. Some of the most influential works in this field are Morris Janowitz, *The Reconstruction of Patriotism: Education for Civic Consciousness* (Chicago: University of Chicago Press, 1983); Yael Tamir, *Liberal Nationalism* (Princeton, NJ: Princeton University Press, 1993); David Miller, *On Nationality* (Oxford: Oxford University Press, 1997); Will Kymlica, *Multicultural Citizenship* (Oxford: Clarendon Press, 1995).

38. See the detailed introduction to William Rogers Brubaker, ed., *Immigration and the Politics of Citizenship in Europe and North America* (Lanham, MD: University Press of America, 1989).

39. Tamir, *Liberal Nationalism*, 129.

40. Some argue that these attachments are necessary for fulfilling other liberal ends. Tamir claims that among the common economic ends, distributive justice is crucially served by a perceived common identity.

41. Eamonn Callan, *Creating Citizens: Political Education and Liberal Democracy* (Oxford: Clarendon Press, 1997). Callan's approach to civic and patriotic education is discussed more extensively in chapter 2.

42. Tamir, *Liberal Nationalism*, 90.

43. Stephen Macedo, *Diversity and Distrust: Civic Education in a Multicultural Democracy* (Cambridge, MA: Harvard University Press, 2000), 3.

44. For a discussion of historical and contemporary ways in which civic society (as well as public and private institutions) generate fear in the national context and benefit from it, see Corey Robin, *Fear: The History of a Political Idea* (New York: Oxford University Press, 2004).

45. Melissa S. Williams, "Citizenship as Identity, Citizenship as Shared Fate, and the Functions of Multicultural Education," in *Citizenship and Education in Liberal-Democratic Societies*, ed. Kevin McDonough and Walter Feinberg (New York: Oxford University Press, 2003), 208–47.

46. Ibid., 218.

47. Ibid., 219.

48. Zygmut Bauman, *Community* (Cambridge, UK: Polity Press, 2001), 4.

49. "Under the auspices of a belligerent nationalism and militarism, community is constructed through shared fears." Henry Giroux, "Democracy, Schooling, and the Culture of Fear after September 11," in *Education as Enforcement*, ed. Kenneth J. Saltman and David A. Gabbard (New York: Routledge Falmer, 2003), ix.

50. For a helpful discussion of political stability and its relations to questions of justice and conflict, see Wayne Norman, "Justice and Stability in Multination States," in *Multinational Democracies*, ed. J. Tully and A. Gagnon (Cambridge: Cambridge University Press, 2001), chap. 3.

51. Williams, "Citizenship as Identity," 231.

52. Rogers Smith, *Stories of Peoplehood* (Cambridge: Cambridge University Press, 2003).

53. Ernest Gellner, *Nations and Nationalism* (Ithaca, NY: Cornell University Press, 1983).

54. Williams, "Citizenship as Identity," 231.

55. Dana Villa, *Socratic Citizenship* (Princeton, NJ: Princeton University Press, 2001).

56. Williams, "Citizenship as Identity," 233.

57. Ibid.

CHAPTER 2
EDUCATION AS WAR BY OTHER MEANS

1. One book that offers a host of cutting-edge psychological research from many countries, performed by scholars from a variety of disciplinary approaches, is the volume edited by Amiram Raviv, Louis Oppenheimer, and Daniel Bar-Tal, *How Children Understand War and Peace* (San Francisco: Jossey-Bass, 1999). The research in this book points to peace as a second-order concept and war as a first-order one, in terms of their acquisition by children. It also substantiates the suggestion that war as a concrete and more visible practice is understood earlier on, and its conception is sustained more stably throughout life than peace, which is a more abstract concept (sometimes understood as a derivation, by negation, of war).

2. In the United States today, as in Israel, the only required unit on civic education is taken in eleventh or, more commonly, twelfth grade and consists mainly of this formal dimension of citizenship.

3. Theda Skocpol, "Will 9/11 and the War on Terror Revitalize American Civic Democracy?" *PS: Political Science and Politics* (September 2002): 537–40, at 537 (emphasis added).

4. See Henry A. Giroux, "Democracy, Freedom, and Justice after September 11th: Rethinking the Role of Educators and the Politics of Schooling," *Teachers College Record* 104:6 (2002): 1138–62.

5. Cecilia O'Leary, *To Die For: The Paradox of American Patriotism* (Princeton, NJ: Princeton University Press, 1999), 221.

6. Ibid., 7.

7. Quoted in Richard M. Ugland, " 'Education for Victory': The High School Victory Corps and Curricular Adaptation during World War II," *History of Education Quarterly* 19:4 (Winter 1979): 435–51, at 436. Note the gender component evident in this statement, which will be explored in chapter 4.

8. Ibid., 437. Similar phenomena have been described in France; see, for example, Stephen L. Harp, *Learning to Be Loyal: Primary Schooling as Nation Building in Alsace and Lorraine, 1850–1940* (DeKalb: Northern Illinois University Press, 1998).

9. John L. Rudolph, *Scientists in the Classroom: The Cold War Reconstruction of American Science Education* (New York: Palgrave, 2002).

10. David H. Parker, " 'The Talent at Its Command': The First World War and the Vocational Aspect of Education, 1914–39," *History of Education Quarterly* 35:3 (Autumn 1995): 237–59, at 237.

11. Daniel Bar-Tal, *The Rocky Road toward Peace* (Jerusalem: Hebrew University Press, 1996) (in Hebrew).

12. Ibid., 14–17.

13. Quoted in the Israeli newspaper *Yediot Aharonot*, August 28, 2003, 1.

14. Quoted in Orit Ichilov, *Education for Citizenship in an Emerging Society* (Tel Aviv: Sifriat Poalim, 1993), 84 (in Hebrew).

15. Ichilov, *Education for Citizenship*, 80.

16. William Galston, "Civic Education in the Liberal State," in *Philosophers on Education: Historical Perspectives*, ed. Amelie Rorty (London: Routledge, 1998), 471. Published earlier in Nancy Rosenblum, ed., *Liberalism and the Moral Life* (Cambridge, MA: Harvard University Press, 1989).

17. Richard Rorty, *Achieving Our Country: Leftist Thought in Twentieth Century America* (Cambridge, MA: Harvard University Press, 1998); Arthur Schlesinger, *The Disuniting of America* (New York: Norton, 1992); Robert Fullinwider, "Patriotic History," in *Multiculturalism and Public Education*, ed. Robert Fullinwider (Cambridge: Cambridge University Press, 1996), 203–30; Eamonn Callan, *Creating Citizens: Political Education and Liberal Democracy* (Oxford: Clarendon Press, 1997).

18. Janowitz, *Reconstruction of Patriotism*, x.

19. Ibid., 8. Note that although Janowitz's book serves as background to my argument, I find it helpful as one of the bases for my argument, I find his book helpful mostly for its historical and analytical characterization of patriotism and civic education. On these dimensions it remains an important work, but its normative dimension, I believe, was outdated by world events, mainly the end of the cold war and the global threat of terrorism (as well as some economic changes). Thus, for example, Janowitz claims that "the goal [of citizenship education] is a world in which war is limited to conventional weapons,

and in which even conventional war is subject to persistent international political inhibition" (11). Although this goal remains a noble one, I find it to be insufficient as a guideline for today's political and civic education.

20. A thorough, critical discussion of these approaches, which includes a psycho-political justification for supporting a sense of community (including national affiliation), is offered in Bernard Yack, "Nation and Individual" (unpublished manuscript), introduction and chap. 2.

21. Harry Brighouse, "Should We Teach Patriotic History?" in *Citizenship and Education in Liberal-Democratic Societies: Teaching for Cosmopolitan Values and Collective Identities*, ed. Kevin McDonough and Walter Feinberg (New York: Oxford University Press 2003), 157–78.

22. Amy Gutmann, *Democratic Education* (Princeton, NJ: Princeton University Press 1999), 312.

23. Amy Gutmann, "Civic Minimalism, Cosmopolitanism and Patriotism: Where Does Democratic Education Stand in Relation to Each?" in *Moral and Political Education*, Nomos 43, ed. Stephen Macedo and Yael Tamir (New York: New York University Press 2002), 23–57, 49.

24. David Miller, *On Nationality* (New York: Oxford University Press, 1997).

25. Yael Tamir, *Liberal Nationalism* (Princeton, NJ: Princeton University Press, 1993).

26. Brighouse calls this argument "the argument from mutual effect."

27. *Education for Democracy*, Albert Shanker Institute, 2003, 3, www.shanker institute.org/downloads/EfD%20final.pdf (accessed June 12, 2005).

28. Ibid., 9.

29. Chester E. Finn Jr., foreword to Diane Ravitch, "A Consumer's Guide to High School History Textbooks," http://www.edexcellence.net/institute/publication/publication.cfm?id–329 (accessed March 2, 2004).

30. Gilbert T. Sewall, *History Textbooks at the New Century* (New York: American Textbooks Council, 2000).

31. Noam Chomsky, *Chomsky on Miseducation*, ed. Donaldo Macedo (Boston: Rowman & Littlefield, 2000), 28.

32. Henry Giroux, *The Abandoned Generation: Democracy Beyond the Culture of Fear* (New York: Palgrave Macmillan, 2003), 25.

33. James Loewen, *Lies My Teachers Told Me: Everything Your American History Textbook Got Wrong* (New York: New Press, 1995).

34. Diane Ravitch, *The Language Police: How Pressure Groups Restrict What Students Learn* (New York: Knopf, 2003).

35. Sheldon M. Stern, *Effective State Standards for U.S. History: A 2003 Report Card*, http://www.edexcellence.net/institute/publication/publication.cfm?id–320#940 (accessed January 4, 2004).

36. *Education for Democracy*, 35.

37. Rogan Kersh, "Civic Engagement and National Belonging," in *Constructing Civic Virtue: A Symposium on the State of American Citizenship* (New York: Campbell Public Affairs Institute, 2003), 1.

38. Brighouse, "Should We Teach Patriotic History?" 165–66.

39. Rorty, *Achieving Our Country*, 11.

40. Gary Nash, Charlotte Crabtree, and Ross E. Dunn, *History on Trial* (New York: Knopf, 1999), 15, quoted in Brighouse, "Should We Teach Patriotic History?"

41. See a critique along similar lines in David Archard, "Should We Teach Patriotism?" *Studies in Philosophy and Education* 18:3 (1999): 157–73.

42. William E. Marsden, " 'Poisoned History': A Comparative Study of Nationalism, Propaganda and the Treatment of War and Peace in the Late Nineteenth- and Early Twentieth-Century School Curriculum," *History of Education* 29:1 (January 2000): 29–49.

43. Jonathan F. Scott, *The Menace of Nationalism in Education* (London: G. Allen & Unwin, 1926), 255.

44. Arthur M. Schlesinger, introduction to A. Walworth, *School Histories at War: A Study of the Treatment of Our Wars in the Secondary School History Books of the United States and in Those of Its Former Enemies* (Cambridge, MA: Harvard University Press, 1938), xiii–xx.

45. Ruth Firer, "The Gordian Knot Between Peace Education and War Education," in *Peace Education: The Concepts, Principles and Practices Around the World*, ed. Gavriel Salomon and Baruch Nevo (Mahwah, NJ: Erlbaum, 2002), 56–62, at 56.

46. For a thorough defense of this argument in the broader social context, see Rogers Smith, *Stories of Peoplehood*.

47. Education Policies Commission, *What the Schools Should Teach in Wartime* (Washington, DC, 1943).

CHAPTER 3
PEACE EDUCATION: ANGER MANAGEMENT AND CARE FOR THE EARTH

1. For contemporary, cross-national evidence of this claim, see *How Children Understand War and Peace*, mainly chap. 1, 2, and 4.

2. Larry Fisk and John Schellenberg, *Patterns of Conflict, Paths to Peace* (Ontario, Canada: Broadview Press, 2000), 161.

3. Johan Galtung, "Violence, Peace, and Peace Research," *Journal of Peace Research* 6:3 (1969): 167–91.

4. "Beliefs about War, Conflict and Peace in Israel as a Function of Developmental, Cultural and Situational Factors," in *How Children Understand War and Peace*, chap. 8.

5. Gavriel Salomon, "The Nature of Peace Education: Not all Programs Are Created Equal," in *Peace Education: The Concepts, Principles and Practices Around the World*, ed. Gavriel Salomon and Baruch Nevo (Mahwah, NJ: Erlbaum, 2002), 3–15, at 6.

6. Ibid., 5.

7. Martha Minow, "Isaac Marks Memorial Lecture: Education for Co-Existence," *Arizona Law Review* 44:1 (2002): 1–29, at 5. The article was later published in Antonia Chayes and Martha Minow, eds., *Imagine Coexistence* (San Francisco: Jossey-Bass, 2003), 213–34. In Minow's account, the United States seems to belong to the latter kind, namely, "more remote from immediate conflict," although she writes after September 11.

8. Minow, "Isaac Marks Memorial Lecture," 5.

9. I argue elsewhere for the teaching of history studies as a way of responding to some of the social challenges of conflict ("Time Is on Our Side: Social Challenges of Democracy at War," unpublished manuscript). History studies is one of the main focal points of expansive education. However, contrary to most of the programs Minow describes, expansive education aims to be a politicized approach rather than an implementation of a dual-focus curriculum alone. In the following chapters, I continue the discussion of how to implement expansive education in the history curriculum.

10. Katherine D. Lane, "Sakha Ukuthula: Facilitating Peace Education with Nonviolence and Justice," *Peace and Change* 45:2 (April 2000): 288–91.

11. See, for example, C. E. Johnson and R. A. Templeton, "Promoting Peace in a Place Called School," *Learning Environments Research* 2:1 (1999): 65–77

12. All the works mentioned in this paragraph refer to articles in Salomon, *Peace Education*.

13. For an appraisal of conflict resolution programs in the United States, see Tricia S. Jones and Daniel Kmitta, eds., *Does It Work? The Case for Conflict Resolution Education in Our Nation's Schools* (Washington, DC: Conflict Resolution Education Network [CREnet], 2000).

14. Minow, "Isaac Marks Memorial Lecture," 5.

15. Ibid., 10.

16. Ifat Maoz, "Multiple Conflicts and Competing Agendas: A Framework for Conceptualizing Structured Encounters Between Groups in Conflict—The Case of a Coexistence Project of Jews and Palestinians in Israel," *Peace and Conflict: A Journal of Peace Psychology*, 6:2 (2000): 135–56.

17. When I say "marginal" I do not necessarily mean "insignificant": one young Palestinian woman who was sent to an Israeli neighborhood as a suicide bomber changed her mind at the last minute and took her deadly baggage back home. She later testified that she recalled a young Israeli woman whom she had met in a "personal encounters" program and was afraid she might kill her. Giving the enemy a name and a face can be influential, but it apparently

does not promote a reevaluation of political perspectives, as even this same anecdote exemplifies.

18. Note that some of these curricular and theoretical discussions are focused not on peace education but on the pragmatics of resolving conflicts among students or within schools in general. See J. Harvey, "Stereotypes and Moral Oversight in Conflict Resolution: What Are We Teaching?" *Journal of Philosophy of Education* 36:4 (2002): 513–27. Many theories refer to "conflict resolution" as part and parcel of the process of educating for peace. One recent book that aims to implement long-term reconciliation methods to enrich the conflict resolution trend's limitations—which are analyzed similarly to the current discussion—is *From Conflict Resolution to Reconciliation*, ed. Yaacov Bar-Siman-Tov (Oxford: Oxford University Press, 2004).

19. This is Joseph Schumpeter's phrase. As this reference hints, this approach is a relative, if only a remote one, of the classical liberal humanist approach. See Joseph Schumpeter, *Imperialism and Social Classes*, trans. by Heinz Norden (New York: Meridian, 1955).

20. Some of the authors that most clearly represent this approach are Birgit Brock-Utne, a Norwegian educational researcher; Betty Reardon, an American scholar who also designs curricular materials for UNESCO; and Ilan Gur-Ze'ev, an Israeli educational philosopher. Some of their publications that are available in English are Birgit Brock-Utne, *Educating for Peace: A Feminist Perspective*, (New York: Pergamon Press, 1985); Betty A. Reardon, *Education for a Culture of Peace in a Gender Perspective* (Paris: UNESCO Publishing, 2001); Ilan Gur-Ze'ev, "Philosophy of Peace Education in a Post-Modern Era," *Educational Theory* 51:3 (2001): 315–36, and *Destroying the Other's Collective Memory* (New York: Lang, 2003).

21. Brock-Utne, *Educating for Peace*, 2.

22. Nancy Rosenblum, introduction to Martha Minow, *Breaking the Cycles of Hatred: Memory, Law and Repair* (Princeton, NJ: Princeton University Press, 2002), 1–13.

23. Ervin Staub, "Notes on Cultures of Violence, Cultures of Caring and Peace, and the Fulfillment of Basic Human Needs," *Political Psychology* 24:1 (2003): 1–13, at 1.

24. For some more radical authors in this trend, like Gur-Ze'ev, a constructive response is practically impossible, as the attempt to educate for peace is in itself a form of oppression, which is a violent act. Hence, it is hard to distinguish the violence of war from violence in a classroom setting where an educator strives to teach peace education materials. Gur-Ze'ev, "Philosophy of Peace Education," 316.

25. Henry Giroux, *The Abandoned Generation: Democracy Beyond the Culture of Fear* (New York: Palgrave Macmillan, 2003), 25.

26. Reardon, *Education for a Culture of Peace*, 12.

27. Ibid., 17.

28. Ibid., 24.

29. Ibid., 78.

30. Ibid., 69–70.

31. Ibid., 187.

32. From the UNESCO second medium-term plan, 1984–1989, quoted in Brock-Utne, *Educating for Peace*, 3.

33. William S. Haft and Elaine R. Weiss, "Peer Mediation in Schools: Expectations and Evaluations," *Harvard Negotiation Law Review* 3 (1998): 213.

34. As Reardon suggests, *Educating for a Culture of Peace*, 85.

35. The Hague Appeal for Peace Civil Society Conference, www. haguepeace.org (accessed June 25, 2005).

36. Ian Harris in Salomon and Nevo, *Peace Education*, 24. Harris offers a detailed peace education approach in Ian M. Harris and Mary Kee Morrison, *Peace Education* (Jefferson, NC: McFarland, 2003).

37. Michael Harbottle and Eiren Harbottle, "The Two Faces of Peace Building," *Journal of Peace and Change* 4:1 (July 1997): 17–28.

38. Boutros Boutros-Ghali, *An Agenda for Peace* (New York: United Nations Department of Public Information, 1995)

39. Michael Walzer, *Arguing About War* (New Haven, CT: Yale University Press, 2004), x.

40. Janowitz, *The Reconstruction of Patriotism*, 74.

41. Giroux is a notable exception—he offers a thorough review of the political context of teaching in wartime; his analysis often is very convincing, although as I suggested, his constructive position too often resembles the holistic approach. Giroux, "Democracy, Freedom and Justice after September 11th."

42. Staub's perspective was discussed here as a unique exception; however, his approach too does not address the sociopolitical consequences of his psychological findings.

43. Minow, "Isaac Marks Memorial Lecture," 8.

CHAPTER 4
FEMINIST CONTRIBUTIONS TO EXPANSIVE EDUCATION

1. Eva Isaksson, ed. *Women and the Military System* (London: Harvester, 1988); Cynthia Enloe, *Bananas, Beaches and Bases: Making Feminist Sense of International Politics* (London: Pandora, 1989); Carolyn Nordstrom, "Women and War: Observations from the Field," *Minerva: Quarterly Report on Women and the Military* 9:1 (Spring 1991); Jeanne Vickers, *Women and War* (London: Zed Books, 1993); Miriam Cooke and Angela Woollacott, eds., *Gendering War Talk* (Princeton, NJ: Princeton University Press, 1993); Karen J. Warren and Duane L. Cady, eds., *Bringing Peace Home: Feminism, Violence and Nature* (Bloomington: Indiana University Press, 1996). For a local gendered perspective of the Israeli-Palestinian conflict, see the impressive collection in Nahla Abdo and Ronit Lentin, eds.,

Women and the Politics of Military Confrontation: Palestinian and Israeli Gendered Narratives of Dislocation (New York: Berghahn Books, 2002).

2. The attempt by some feminists to put aside the question of war as irrelevant to feminist interests is unwarranted. War has too strong an impact on women's lives to justify a refusal to theorize it.

3. United Nations Web site, www.un.org (accessed September 14, 2004).

4. *Hypatia* devoted an issue to contemporary discussions on the problem of evil. Some of the essays discuss gendered aspects of war. See *Hypatia* 18:1 (2003): Debra Bergoffen, "February 22, 2001: Toward a Politics of the Vulnerable Body," 116–34; Mary Anne Franks, "Obscene Undersides: Women and Evil between the Taliban and the United States," 135–56.

5. For an excellent debate on "right to fight" feminism versus antimilitarist feminism, seen through the lens of citizenship rights, see Ilene Rose Feinman, *Citizenship Rites: Feminist Soldiers and Feminist Antimilitarists* (New York: New York University Press, 2000).

6. Joshua S. Goldstein, *War and Gender: How Gender Shapes the War System and Vice Versa* (Cambridge: Cambridge University Press, 2001).

7. Jean Elshtain, *Women and War* (Chicago: University of Chicago Press 1995).

8. Sara Ruddick, "The Moral Horror of the September Attacks," *Hypatia* 18:1 (2003): 212–22.

9. See, for example, Gideon Alon and Amos Harel, "Female Soldier Charged with Making Palestinian Woman Drink Poison" *Ha'aretz*, June 23, 2003, A4.

10. Cynthia Enloe, *Maneuvers: The International Politics of Militarizing Women's Lives* (Berkeley: University of California Press, 2000); and as discussed in the previous chapter, Brock-Utne, *Educating for Peace*.

11. Goldstein, *War and Gender*, 127.

12. Elizabeth Prugl, "Gender and War: Causes, Constructions, and Critique," *Perspectives on Politics* 1:2 (June 2003): 335–42, at 335.

13. Elizabeth Kier, "Uniform Justice: Assessing Women in Combat," *Perspectives on Politics* 1:2 (June 2003): 343–47, at 343.

14. For a review of the ways in which war affects media coverage and public debate in the media, see Matthew A. Baum, *Soft News Goes to War: Public Opinion and American Foreign Policy in the New Media Age* (Princeton, NJ: Princeton University Press, 2003). A recent critical sociological survey of the civic effects of militarism on Israeli society can be found in Yagil Levy, *A Different Army for Israel: Materialistic Militarism in Israel* (Tel Aviv: Yediot Aharonot, 2003) (in Hebrew).

15. Nel Noddings, *Caring: A Feminine Approach to Ethics and Moral Education* (Berkeley: University of California Press, 1984), 183.

16. William J. Bennett, *Why We Fight: Moral Clarity and the War on Terrorism* (New York: Doubleday, 2002). For a liberal discussion on the same topic, see Chris Hadges, *War Is a Force that Gives Us Meaning* (New York: Anchor Books,

2002). See a feminist critique of Bennett's perspective in Bat-ami Bar On, "Manly After-Effects of September 11, 2001," *International Journal of Feminist Politics* 5:3 (November 2003): 456–58.

17. Dafna Izraeli, Ariella Friedman, Henriette Dahan-Kalev, Sylvie Fogel-Bijaovi, Hanna Herzog, Manar Hasan, and Hannah Nave, eds., *Sex, Gender, Politics* (Tel-Aviv: Hakibutz Hameuhad, 1999) (in Hebrew).

18. Susan Moller Okin, "Feminism, Women's Human Rights, and Cultural Differences," *Hypatia* 13:3 (1998): 32–52, at 36.

19. Iris Marion Young, "Feminist Reactions to the Contemporary Security Regime," *Hypatia* 18:1 (2003): 223–31.

20. Cynthia Enloe, "Beyond 'Rambo': Women and the Varieties of Militarized Masculinity," in *Women and the Military System*, ed. Eva Isaksson (London: Harvester, 1988).

21. One such ad hoc lesson plan, prepared hastily by the school district of Philadelphia after the Iraq war began, is *Conflict and Crisis*. It combines geographic and ethnic facts about Iraq with tips on coping with stress. It does not discuss any political aspect of the conflict, or even the conflict itself, but is designed more as a basic resource for learning about the region. I thank Kathy Schultz for telling me about this lesson plan and for valuable discussion on its civic and gendered aspects.

22. Pearl M. Oliner and Samuel P. Oliner, *Toward a Caring Society: Ideas into Action* (Westport, CT: Praeger, 1995); Deborah Eaker-Rich and Jane Van Galen, eds., *Caring in an Unjust World: Negotiating Borders in Schools* (Albany: State University of New York Press, 1996); Betty Reardon and Eva Nordland, eds., *Learning Peace: The Promise of Ecological and Cooperative Education* (Albany: State University of New York Press, 1994).

23. Sara Ruddick, *Maternal Thinking: Toward a Politics of Peace* (Boston: Beacon Press, 1989).

24. Ibid., 145.

25. The most important perspective on the ethics of care and its implications to educational and pedagogic practices is found in the work of Nel Noddings. See, for example, Noddings, *Caring*. A more concrete discussion of the implication of her approach to schooling can be found in Nel Noddings, *The Challenge to Care in Schools: An Alternative Approach to Education* (New York: Teachers College Press, 1992). Although I find her moral and educational approach appealing both theoretically and practically, her reliance on gender differences in these works is somewhat essentialist, a perspective that she does not endorse in her later writings. Still, some of the suggestions she makes about schooling can be adapted to expansive education regardless of their essentialist justification.

26. bell hooks, *Teaching to Transgress: Education and the Practice of Freedom* (New York: Routledge, 1994); *Talking Back: Thinking Feminist, Thinking Black* (Boston: South End Press, 1989).

27. Sara Ruddick, "Notes Toward a Feminist Peace Politics," in *Gendering War Talk*, 109–27, at 109.

28. Brock-Utne, *Educating for Peace*, 73.

29. Noddings, *Caring*.

30. This concept was suggested by Jane Roland Martin and later employed by various feminist philosophers of education. For a rich account of this perspective, see the articles in the volume edited by Ann Diller, Barbara Houston, Kathryn Pauly Morgan, and Maryann Ayim, *The Gender Question in Education: Theory, Pedagogy and Politics* (Boulder, CO: Westview, 1996).

31. For a thorough discussion of these tools from a radical perspective, see Paulo Freire and Ira Shor, *A Pedagogy of Liberation* (New York: Palgrave Macmillan, 1987); for a feminist perspective, see Diana Fuss, *Essentially Speaking: Feminism, Nature and Difference* (New York: Routledge, 1989).

32. The combination of caring emotions and cognitive engagement was most effectively put forth again by Nel Noddings. For a general outline of this approach, see Nel Noddings, "An Ethics of Care and Its Implications for Instructional Arrangements," in *The Education Feminism Reader*, ed. Lynda Stone (New York: Routledge, 1994). For a more detailed perspective on emotions and cognition in class, see an excellent article by Kathryn Pauly Morgan, "The Perils and Paradoxes of the Bearded Mothers," in *The Gender Question in Education*.

33. Elizabeth J. Tisdell, *Creating Inclusive Adult Learning Environments: Insights from Multicultural Education and Feminist Pedagogy* (Collingdale, PA: DIANE Publishing, 1995).

34. Ruddick, in *Gendering War Talk*, 122.

Chapter 5
Multicultural Education: Acknowledgment and Forgiveness

1. Susan Moller Okin, *Is Multiculturalism Bad for Women?* (Princeton, NJ: Princeton University Press, 1999), 4.

2. Amy Gutmann, *Democratic Education*, 2nd ed. (Princeton, NJ: Princeton University Press, 1999), 304–5. Gutmann demonstrates that at least in the field of public education, the two options are not mutually exclusive.

3. Michael Walzer, *On Toleration* (New Haven, CT: Yale University Press, 1997).

4. Some authors argue that this indeed is also an argument against privatizing the relations between society and subgroups within it. I do not attempt to tackle this issue here, for the notion of tolerance as an educational guideline remains less useful for the purposes of expansive education.

5. Charles Taylor, *Multiculturalism*, ed. Amy Gutmann (Princeton, NJ: Princeton University Press, 1994), 25.

6. For a recent thorough discussion of a vast array of such claims, see Duncan Ivison, *Postcolonial Liberalism* (Cambridge: Cambridge University Press, 2003).

7. Trudy Govier, "What Is Acknowledgement and Why Is It Important?" in *Dilemmas of Reconciliation*, ed. Carol A. L. Prager and Trudy Govier (Ontario, Canada: Wilfrid Laurier University Press, 2003), 71.

8. Multiple perspectives on the distinction between seeking truth and seeking reparations or punishment in the context of the TRC are available in Robert I. Rotberg and Dennis Thompson, eds., *Truth v. Justice: The Morality of Truth Commissions* (Princeton, NJ: Princeton University Press, 2000). See particularly David A. Crocker, "Truth Commissions, Transitional Justice, and Civil Society," 99–121.

9. Govier, "What is Acknowledgment?" 82.

10. This is the tendency in various trends of patriotic education, as critically discussed in Harry Brighouse, "Should We Teach Patriotic History?"

11. An interesting example of one such history textbook can be seen in Joy Hakim's series, *A History of US* (New York: Oxford University Press, 1999). See the discussion in Gutmann, *Democratic Education*, 307.

12. James Banks, *Education in the Eighties: Multiethnic Education* (Washington, DC: National Education Association, 1981).

13. James Banks, "Multicultural Education: Characteristics and Goals," in *Multicultural Education: Issues and Perspectives*, ed. J. Banks and C. Banks (Boston: Allyn & Bacon, 1989). For a more recent account of multiculturalism around the world, see James Banks, *Diversity and Citizenship Education: Global Perspectives* (San Francisco: Jossey-Bass, 2003).

14. Bhikhu Parekh, *Rethinking Multiculturalism* (Cambridge, MA: Harvard University Press, 2000), 227.

15. Ibid., 229.

16. The Freire approach to libratory education stresses the constructivity of innovative pedagogic approaches, such as the dialogical approach, to challenging social issues. See Paulo Freire and Ira Shor, *A Pedagogy of Liberation*. Coleman suggested that the liberal civic education task could be undertaken more effectively and less confrontationally if done through pedagogic rather than curricular changes (following the *Mozert* controversy). See Joe Coleman, "Civic Pedagogies and Liberal-Democratic Curricula," *Ethics* 108:4 (1998): 746–61. These are examples of the importance of pedagogic approaches to the introduction of civic-democratic values.

17. Michael Ignatieff makes this claim in the context of the Balkan wars in *The Warrior's Honour: Ethnic War and the Modern Conscience* (New York: Penguin, 1997).

18. See most recently the debate in the *Journal of Philosophy of Education*: Patricia White, "What Should We Teach Children about Forgiveness?" *Journal of Philosophy of Education* 36:1 (2002): 57–67; L. P. Barnes, "Forgiveness, the Moral Law and Education: A Reply to Patricia White," *Journal of Philosophy of Education* 36:4 (2002): 519–34; Marianna Papastephanou, "Forgiving and Requesting Forgiveness," *Journal of Philosophy of Education* 37:3 (2003): 503–24.

19. Some of the prominent examples are Jean Hampton and Jeffrie Murphy, *Forgiveness and Mercy* (Cambridge: Cambridge University Press, 1988); Avishai Margalit, *The Ethics of Memory* (Cambridge, MA: Harvard University Press, 2002); Martha Minow, *Breaking the Cycles of Hatred: Memory, Law and Repair* (Princeton, NJ: Princeton University Press, 2002); Susan Brison, *Aftermath and the Remaking of a Self* (Princeton, NJ: Princeton University Press, 2002); Joram Graf Haber, *Forgiveness* (Lanham, MD: Rowman & Littlefield, 1991).

20. Jacques Derrida, *On Cosmopolitanism and Forgiveness* (London: Routledge, 2001), 28.

21. Ibid., 32.

22. Hannah Arendt, *The Human Condition* (Chicago: University of Chicago Press, 1998), 212–23.

23. Michael Donald, a black teenager in Mobile, Alabama, was abducted, tortured, and killed in a Ku Klux Klan plot. A lawsuit brought by his mother, Beulah Mae Donald, later resulted in a landmark judgment that bankrupted one Klan organization and significantly influenced the membership and actions of others. See case number 84–0725, USDC Southern District of Alabama.

24. Tara Smith, "Tolerance and Forgiveness: Virtues or Vices?" *Journal of Applied Philosophy* 14:1 (1997): 31–41.

25. White, "What Should We Teach Children about Forgiveness?"

26. Ibid., 64.

27. Ibid., 66.

28. Papastephanou, "Forgiving and Requesting Forgiveness," 516.

29. For a competing model of forgiveness that represents the incompatibility of a relaxed model to the Jewish and Israeli context, see Margalit, *The Ethics of Memory*. I thank Nicole Behnam, a graduate student and educational activist, for a discussion on the irrelevance of a relaxed model of forgiveness in the context of the Balkan wars and certain African cultures such as the one in Sierra Leone, which espouses views of forgiveness which differ significantly from the Abrahamic traditions.

30. See a critique of "cheap grace" as a degradation of the Christian view on forgiveness in Dietrich Bonhoeffer, *Works*, vol. 4, *Discipleship*, also published as *The Cost of Discipleship*, ed. John Godsey and Geffrey B. Kelly, trans. Barbara Green and Reinhard Krauss (Minneapolis: Fortress Press, 2000).

31. See President George W. Bush's apology in Senegal: "Speaking in Senegal today, President Bush acknowledged that America was wrong for her involvement in the slave trade," http://www.msnbc.com/news/936376 .asp?cp1–1 (accessed July 27, 2003).

The Canadian government has been pondering similar acts in regard to various discriminations performed by the government in the past. See an official document of the Advisory Committee of the Secretary of State, http://www.pch.gc.ca/progs/multi/wcar/advisory/redress_e.shtml (accessed November 21, 2003). A similar act of formal request for forgiveness was made by

Prime Minister Barak of Israel to the Sephardic Jewish community for decades-long discrimination against them by governmental institutions.

32. Papastephanou, "Forgiving and Requesting Forgiveness," 522.

33. There are clear exceptions to this claim—slavery and Nazism are ready examples—but in most conflicts both sides can be identified as guilty of at least some wrongdoing, and thus the expectation from all to consider their contribution to past or present conflicts is relevant.

34. Theodor W. Adorno, "What Does Coming to Terms with the Past Mean?" in *Bitburg in Moral and Political Perspective*, ed. Geoffrey Hartman, trans. Timothy Bahti and Geoffrey Hartman (Bloomington: Indiana University Press, 1986) (originally published 1959).

35. Calhoun Cheshire, "Changing One's Heart" *Ethics* 103 (1992): 76–96.

36. See chapter 2.

37. Margalit, *The Ethics of Memory*, 208. See also the discussion on memory and being forgiven in Cheshire, "Changing One's Heart."

38. Margalit, *The Ethics of Memory*, 74; Minow, *Education for Co-existence*.

39. Austin Sarat reminds us that reflecting on the universality of death may help us transcend the urge to revenge hateful crimes. Austin Sarat, "When Memory Speaks: Remembrance and Revenge in *Unforgiven*," in Minow, *Breaking the Cycles of Hatred*, 236–52.

CHAPTER 6
EXPANSIVE EDUCATION

1. Michael Ignatieff, *The Lesser Evil* (Princeton, NJ: Princeton University Press, 2004), 9.

2. As described most prominently in Michael Walzer, *Just and Unjust Wars* (Princeton, NJ: Princeton University Press, 1977).

3. See, for example, Gutmann, *Democratic Education*; Stephen Macedo, "Liberal Civic Education and Religious Fundamentalism: The Case of God v. John Rawls?" *Ethics* 105:3 (1995): 468–96; William Galston, *Liberal Purposes* (Cambridge: Cambridge University Press, 1991); Iris Marion Young, "Mothers, Citizenship and Independence: A Critique of Pure Family Values," *Ethics* 105:3 (1995): 535–56.

4. See examples of one such perspective in Mark Holmes, "Education and Citizenship in an Age of Pluralism," in *Making Good Citizens: Education and Civil Society*, ed. Diane Ravitch and Joseph P. Viteritti (New Haven, CT: Yale University Press, 2001), 187–212. For a more strictly libertarian conception of education, which includes the total rejection of public funding for education and hopes for a free market education as the source of democratic educational practice, see James Tooley, *Reclaiming Education* (New York: Cassell, 2000). A critical discussion of education for "privatized democracy" can be found in

David T. Sehr, *Education for Public Democracy* (New York: State University of New York Press, 1997), 9–107.

5. David Sehr presents the two conceptions as clearly distinct, as does Diane Ravitch and other authors. A careful reading may reveal that beyond the clear ends of the spectrum of the debate—say, Tooley on the libertarian side and Chomsky on the radical side—most authors express a strong commitment to democratic values, to the introduction of democratic institutions, and to creating the basis for democratic commitments. Emphasis and focus vary, of course, but the similarities are significant as well.

6. The seminal work presenting what are now widely held conceptions of civic disengagement is Robert Putnam, *Making Democracy Work* (Princeton, NJ: Princeton University Press, 1993). The work that began the current debate on civic engagement in the United States is Robert Putnam, "Bowling Alone: The decline of Social Capital in America," *Journal of Democracy* 6:1 (Summer 1997): 129–40, and in the educational context, Robert Putnam, "Community-Based Social Capital and Educational Performance," in *Making Good Citizens*, 58–95.

7. Katherine Kersten, "What Is 'Education for Democracy'?" in *Terrorists, Despots and Democracy: What Our Children Need to Know* (Washington, DC: Thomas B. Fordham Foundation, 2003). The document is also available online at http://www.edexcellence.net/foundation/publication/publication .cfm?id–316#836 (accessed November 11, 2004).

8. Ibid.

9. Dana Vila, in *Socratic Citizenship* (Princeton, NJ: Princeton University Press, 2001), suggests that this line of argument for citizenship, consisting of a commitment to serve a greater good as exemplified by virtues and acts, marks the Aristotelian tradition in Western political thought. As an alternative, he offers a critical conception of philosophic citizenship based on the Socratic tradition, the focus of which is on the individual's ability to negate given social conventions. His perception of democratic citizenship converges in some respects with the one that informs expansive education.

10. See additionally many authors in the same volume (*Terrorists, Despots and Democracy*), in particular Lamar Alexander and William Galston.

11. Norman Nie and D. Sunshine Hylligus, "Education and Democratic Citizenship," in *Making Good Citizens*, 30–57, at 30.

12. For a discussion of contemporary research on this question, which supports the claim that civic education is a critical tool in reversing the trend of youth political disengagement, see William Galston, "Civic Knowledge, Civic Education and Civic Engagement: A Summary of Recent Research," in *Constructing Civic Virtue: A Symposium on the State of American Citizenship* (New York: Campbell Public Affairs Institute, 2003), 33–58.

13. A main study on this topic is Michael Delli Carpini and Scott Keeter, *What Americans Know about Politics and Why It Matters* (New Haven, CT: Yale University Press, 1996). Other contemporary examples include William Gal-

ston, "Civic Education and Political Participation," *Phi Delta Kappan* 85:1 (2003): 29–33; and Judith Torney-Purta, "The School's Role in Developing Civic Engagement: A Study of Adolescents in Twenty-Eight Countries," *Applied Developmental Science* 6:4 (2002): 202–11. Note that although these studies measure in various ways the marked effectiveness of civic education, the standards movement and in particular No Child Left Behind are pushing schools away from civic studies. Thus, despite evidence of the direct contribution of civic education to civic engagement and participation, civic studies today in many states in the United States is confined to one course in twelfth grade. To compare, in December 2004 the Israeli Ministry of Education suggested eliminating the requisite of civic studies from the list of external final exams required to achieve a high school diploma.

14. The interest in news is also reflective of the moralistic and simplistic framing of war, which further diminishes public debate. For a thorough debate, including data on interest in news during military and other crises, see Baum, *Soft News Goes to War*, mainly chap. 2 and 4.

15. Following Hannah Arendt's discussion of political judgment in Seyla Benhabib, *Situating the Self: Gender, Community and Postmodernism in Contemporary Ethics* (New York: Routledge, 1992), 192.

16. Williams, "Citizenship as Identity," in McDonough and Feinberg, *Citizenship and Education*, 237.

17. Empirical evidence on how perspectives are silenced are discussed in E. Noelle-Neumann, *The Spiral of Silence: Public Opinion—Our Social Skin* (Chicago: University of Chicago Press, 1984).

18. Gutmann, *Democratic Education*.

19. Ibid., 292.

20. Amy Gutmann, "Challenges of Multiculturalism in Democratic Education," *Philosophy of Education Yearbook 1995*.

21. See, for example, K. Anthony Appiah, "Cosmopolitan Patriots," in *For Love of Country: Debating the Limits of Patriotism*, ed. Martha Nussbaum (Boston: Beacon Press, 1996), 22.

22. *Mozert v. Hawkins City Board of Education*, 484 U.S. 1066.

23. Gutmann, *Democratic Education*, 294.

24. For a persuasive argument for diversity as a means of preserving democracy, also referring to its role in times of conflict, see Ronald David Glass, "Pluralism, Justice, Democracy and Education: Conflict and Citizenship," *Philosophy of Education Yearbook 2003*.

25. Gutmann, *Democratic Education*, 309.

26. Henry A. Giroux, "Democracy, Freedom, and Justice after September 11th," 1155.

27. See Meira Levinson, "Separate but Equal? Segregated Schools and the Fragmentation of Civic Narrative" (presentation), American Political Science Association, Chicago, IL, September 1, 2004.

Index

Abrahamic tradition, 104–5; apologizing and, 108–9; forgiveness and, 146n29
Abu Graib scandal, 79
acknowledgment, 93–94, 95, 119, 126–27; diversity and, 126–27; justifying reverse patriotism, 99–103; of past wrongs, 96–99, 108–9, 146–47n31
Adorno, Theodor, 109
African Americans, recognition of injustice against, 109
Albert Shanker Institute study, 48–49
anger management approach, 61, 70
anti-war education, versus peace education, 58–59
apartheid regime, acknowledgment of, 99
apology, public, 108–9; just forgiveness and, 111–12
Arab Americans, distrustful perception of, 26–27
Arato, Andrew, 20
Arendt, Hannah, 105
Aristotelian tradition, 148n9

Balkan wars, forgiveness and, 146n29
Banks, James, 100
Bar-Tal, Daniel, 40, 135n1
Barak, Prime Minister, request for forgiveness by, 146–47n31
Barzilai, Gad, 131n10
Beauvoir, Simone de, 85
belligerent citizenship, 2–3, 5, 9; challenges of to democracies, 31–32; versus citizenship as shared fate, 30–31; constructive aspects of, 68; cultivation of in Israeli education system, 40–43; diversity and, 24–25; drawbacks of, 20; expansive education response to, 113–29; features of, 11–16; Israeli versus U.S. experience of, 12–13, 16–22; making of, 36–39; national identity and, 23–32, 116–17; patriarchal culture and, 91–92;

public education and, 122–23; security issues and in Israel, 132–33n17; short-term needs of, 53–54; taught in public education system, 33–35, 82–84; as threat to democratic principles, 131n9; women's status and, 77–80
Benhabib, Seyla, 121–22
Bennett, William, 81
Bin-Laden, Osama, 50–51
Bonhoeffer, Dietrich, 146n30
Borelli, Mario, 65
Bosnian self-identity, 98
Brighouse, Harry, 44–45, 51–52, 145n10
Britain, wartime vocational education in, 39
Brock-Utne, Birgit, 65, 88, 140n20
Bush, George W., 146n31; changing international policies of, 18; national unity behind, 20; and response to September 11 attack, 13–14

Callan, Eamonn, 23, 25–26, 46, 47
Canada, acknowledgment of past wrongs by, 146–47n31
care, ethics of, 143n25, 144n32
censorship, 15–16
Chacekorkalo, Dinka, 61
character ideal, 117
Chomsky, Noam, 49, 148n5
Christian forgiveness, 104–5, 107, 146n30
church-state separation, 39
citizen-warriors, educating, 55–56. *See also* military; soldiers
citizenship: acquiring, 23–24; American, 38; changing conceptions of, 2–3, 4–5, 10, 34–35; as communal identity, 116–17; diverse views of, 148n9; ethnonationalist, 16; gendered notion of, 133–34n30; individual-state power balance and, 9–10; liberal, 16; multiculturalism and, 28; multidimensional description

154